Bayford

The First One Hundred Years

Nigel Watson

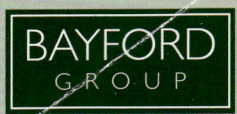

First published in 2021 in Great Britain
on behalf of Bayford & Co Ltd by
St Matthew's Press,
10, St Matthew's Terrace, Leyburn,
North Yorkshire DL8 5EL
www.corporatehistories.org.uk

ISBN 978-1-8383994-1-2

Design and artwork by Brian Glanfield
Printed and bound by Pureprint Group
Bellbrook Park, Uckfield, East Sussex TN22 1PL

Contents

Forewords

It is my pleasure to introduce you to the 100 year history of Bayford & Co Ltd. In doing so, I want to thank all my many colleagues both past and present for their contribution to the success of the company.

Particular mention must go to my father, Frederick Turner, who joined the company in 1922 as an office boy, aged sixteen. Having worked his way up steadily through some very difficult years in the coal industry, he benefited from one of the earliest share option schemes as by 1968 he had acquired 50% ownership of the company.

My dear late brother, David Turner, with whom I worked for over forty years, wanted to expand and diversify, which father resisted until I joined the company as Financial Director. David and I purchased the remaining 50% four years later.

David was a great sales and marketing person and although I had very contrasting skills, we complemented each other. We enjoyed many high points and some low ones over the years; always sharing everything equally.

David's son, Jonathan, has expertly managed the Group's growth and diversity since acquiring the business in 2004 and I wish him and his team continued success in the future.

John Turner

You make your own luck. I have been very, very lucky. I have only worked at Bayford for a third of its wonderfully dynamic life, though I have been lucky to have known a great many hard working, funny and inspiring people and personalities.

I am thankful that my father and uncle gave me a job and saw in me the creative sales person I wanted to be. I am thankful that around the same time they also employed Liz Slater (nee Hill) who has inspired so many at Bayford with me and has been the steady rock of common sense I often needed. When I was young, my father once told me that I would never be as successful as him. It continuously saddens me that he is not here now so we can have that discussion again. It helps having my Uncle John at Bowcliffe and we often share stories of the characters from the old days.

Working in a family business can be incredibly challenging. We have had some very delicate and emotional moments over the years and I am grateful for those around us who put up with them. I have always believed that Bayford as a business should continue to grow and develop for the long term benefit of all those who care about it and work hard for the future success. Some who have contributed to this book have worked for Bayford for decades, quite a few for over 30 years. That tells me we are doing something right.

I owe a debt of gratitude to everyone who has taken time out of their busy lives to help Nigel write this story, especially to my wife Karen who has put up with a great deal over the years. She has always been there behind the scenes working tirelessly and patiently. Bringing up three young children on the journey hasn't been easy. A huge thank you goes especially to Lorraine my PA who lives with me every day trying to make order out of extreme chaos. Thank you all from the bottom of my heart. I am very lucky: if you think you can, you will.

Jonathan Turner

Acknowledgements

This project has been driven by Jonathan Turner's enthusiasm for the history of the group. He has been unfailingly helpful and given freely of his time to sit down and talk about his own recollections of the business. John Turner too helped me to fill in many gaps, gave generously of his time to talk about his involvement with Bayford and also commented on the draft. Lorraine Lowe not only shared with me her own reminiscences but also was invaluable in tracking down interviewees, arranging interviews, retrieving information and reviewing the draft history. I am very grateful to them all. I would also like to thank the following who kindly talked to me about Bayford: Lindsay Austin, Ken Gardiner, Sally Genn, Tim Hall, David and Debbie Hobson, Mark Kilvington, Bob McNaughton, Julie O'Shaughnessy, Chris Ritchie, Tony Sharp, Liz Slater, James Spencer, Rob Staines and Karen Turner.

Nigel Watson

Bayford

1

Any visitor arriving at Bowcliffe Hall, Bayford's beautiful head office near Wetherby in Yorkshire, would almost immediately get a sense of the man behind the business. One of the first things the visitor sees on driving through the gates is the statue of a small girl standing on the lawn gazing up at a sign in front of her. The visitor sees first of all the other side of the sign, which orders, 'No Stopping: No Parking: No Kidding'. But on the side attracting the girl's attention is a quote from *Alice in Wonderland*, for the girl is indeed Alice:

'I don't want to go amongst mad people,' Alice remarked.

'Oh, you can't help that,' said the Cat. 'We are all mad here. I'm mad, you're mad.'

'How do you know I'm mad?' said Alice.

'You must be,' said the Cat, 'or you wouldn't have come here.'

It sums up in part Jonathan Turner's view of the type of business environment he wanted to create, one populated by people who were fun to work with, who were a little bit different, a little bit quirky, a little bit mad. It is this ethos that has been behind the success of the business for the past 30 years.

The Turner family has been involved with Bayford since it was founded after the First World War. Perhaps the common thread through much of that history has been energy and indeed for a time the business was known as Bayford Energy. It began by selling coal; today it sells gas and electricity. And in this shift lies one reason why the Bayford name has survived: the business has adapted constantly to changing circumstances. Jonathan's father,

David, began moving the business away from coal in the 1960s when Bayford began distributing oil and selling petrol. In the 1970s and 1980s, his dream was the creation of an integrated energy business. Although this had mixed results, it helped to insure the company against the uncertain fortunes of the coal industry. In the late 1990s, as Jonathan took a leading role, Bayford overcame the crisis in fuel retailing by teaming up with a national fuel bunkering partner and entering the fuel card sector. Latterly, the company's approach has been characterised by keeping an open mind about the future of any of its businesses, happy either to expand them by applying its expertise in acquisitions and management, or to sell them if an appropriate offer comes along. Most recently, echoing the decision to move from coal into oil, Bayford has moved from oil into gas and electricity.

Another reason for Bayford's longevity is the way its leaders have complemented each other in their skills. Although we know little about the relationship Fred Turner, Jonathan's grandfather, had with the company's founding chairman, Benjamin Binks, it might not be too far away from the truth to say that Fred's skills in managing the business day-to-day were complemented by the wider overview of the business taken by Benjamin as chairman for so many years. David Turner and his brother John formed, by all accounts, an ideal partnership; David was an extrovert, full of ideas, the epitome of the salesman; and John was a calming influence, looking after the details in which David was less interested. For the last 30

years, it is the partnership between Jonathan Turner and Liz Slater that has driven the business; Jonathan, his father writ large in many of his traits; Liz, the pragmatist, translating Jonathan's vision into practice.

Furthermore, certainly since the days of David and John Turner, people have enjoyed coming to work for the company. By and large, Bayford's leaders have enthused their teams, creating commitment, dedication and loyalty. The key has been avoiding complacency and inertia, and under Jonathan and Liz the company's ethos of working hard and having fun was not only reinvigorated but also promoted more overtly. In addition, they have shown good judgement in recruiting and developing talented young people, who have filled senior positions and formed the support team that has been necessary for the development of the business.

Lastly, ownership has never been sacrosanct. Bayford is and isn't a family business. It has been re-born with every passing generation. It wasn't a family business to start with in terms of ownership even though it was always managed by the Turner family. Fred Turner only ever had half the shares in the business and it didn't pass completely into the family until David and John bought it in 1972. That was a brave decision by the brothers, as was Jonathan Turner's decision to buy the business from them a generation later.

The story that follows charts the ups and downs of a business and a family whose fortunes have been intertwined for a century.

1919-37

2

How it all began

The company takes its name from Bayford, a small village in Hertfordshire. It was here, so the story goes, that the firm's founders agreed to join up to form a new business. This must be true since there is no other reason why the company should take the name it still carries today.

The four founders, Frank Baker, Benjamin Binks, William Chambers and Sidney Ludolf, were near neighbours in Headingley, Leeds. During the First World War they all saw service on the Western Front. Benjamin Binks and William Chambers fought alongside each other in the Army Service Corps while Frank Baker served in the 5th Battalion of the King's Own Yorkshire Light Infantry. They all landed in France in April 1915 and may well have stopped off in Bayford on the journey. Sidney Ludolf, however, was already in the United States and joined the conflict only when America entered the war in 1917. He then went back to the US, returning to Leeds in 1921.

Bayford, Hertfordshire.

The Founders

Bayford & Co was founded by four young men from Leeds: Frank Baker, born in 1884; Sidney Ludolf, born in 1887; Benjamin Binks, born in 1889; and William Chambers, born in 1890. **Frank Baker** was the son of an Essex clergyman. After leaving school he joined an insurance company and in 1914 he was working in Leeds as an insurance inspector. **Sydney Ludolf** came from an old-established Jewish family who ran a prosperous textile business in Leeds. As a younger son, there was no room for Sydney in the family firm and instead he trained as an architect. **Benjamin Binks** was the son of an insurance agent who had married into money. This allowed Benjamin's father to give up work and educate his son at Sedbergh School. Benjamin then returned to Leeds to study law. **William Chambers' father** was the National Telephone Company's superintendent in Leeds. Entrepreneurial by nature, William became a partner in a firm making iron buildings.

With all four living in Headingley, they probably knew each other before the war. By then, Sydney was living and working in the United States. Frank, Benjamin and William all joined up when war was declared. Frank served with the King's Own Yorkshire Light Infantry; Benjamin and William, with the West Riding Divisional Train of the Army Service Corps, all of them landing in France in April 1915, all of them ending the war as officers. Remarkably, Sydney, who was still a British citizen, joined them when the USA entered the war in 1917, coming to France as a corporal in the US Army's 3rd Infantry Division, serving with Field Hospital No. 7.

All four would return to live permanently in Leeds. Although they never took an active role in managing the business, they and their descendants remained shareholders after the business was incorporated in 1937 until its sale to David and John Turner in 1972.

The Army Service Corps on the Western Front: a supply train steaming into a railhead at Frechencourt, March 1917.
(© IWM (Q4820))

Men of the King's Own Yorkshire Light Infantry fusing mortar bombs, Wieltjie, near Ypres, 1 October 1917.
(© IWM (Q6454))

At different times the company has claimed that it was founded in 1919, 1920 and 1922, and there is no firm evidence of the actual date. But if the story of three young soldiers making a pact en route to war is true, then it seems reasonable to take 1919 as the date, for why would they wait any longer to set up their new venture?

Since all four founders were pursuing independent careers, it might seem odd for them to set up a business as coal merchants. It seems to have been a sideline since none of them was involved in running the business day-to-day. There were, however, good reasons for them to choose the coal industry. In the inter-war years, it was still one of the country's most important industries.

Early Years

Leeds was as good a place as any to start a business selling coal. Unlike many other regional centres, it was not as badly hit as others by the inter-war depression. As well as a

The Coal Industry

Although the founders of Bayford & Co had no experience of the coal industry, their decision to set up in business as coal merchants reflected the fact that coal was still one of the country's most important industries. As the founders marched off to war in 1914, the industry, it was said, was 'the greatest of the British trades'. It employed more than 1.1 million miners producing 287 million tons of coal every year, a total never again exceeded. Coal heated homes and offices, drove railway engines, powered ocean-going liners and fired up the furnaces of steel and ironworks. Forests of chimneys sprouted from the rooftops of many towns and cities; buildings were blackened by soot; and dense, choking smogs became a regular affliction during cold autumn and winter days. Yorkshire alone had more than 100 pits, which were regarded as among the most efficient in the industry. Until nationalisation in 1947, each pit sold its coal via agents, presenting opportunities for Bayford & Co, well-served in Leeds by direct rail transport from the pits or via barges along the Aire & Calder Navigation.

Bullcroft Colliery, Carcroft, a typical Yorkshire colliery of the 1920s. (Derne Valley/Alamy)

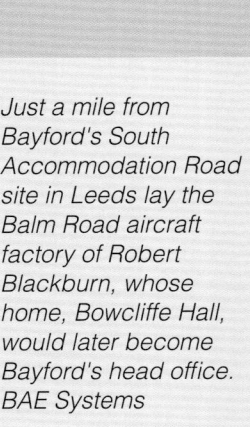

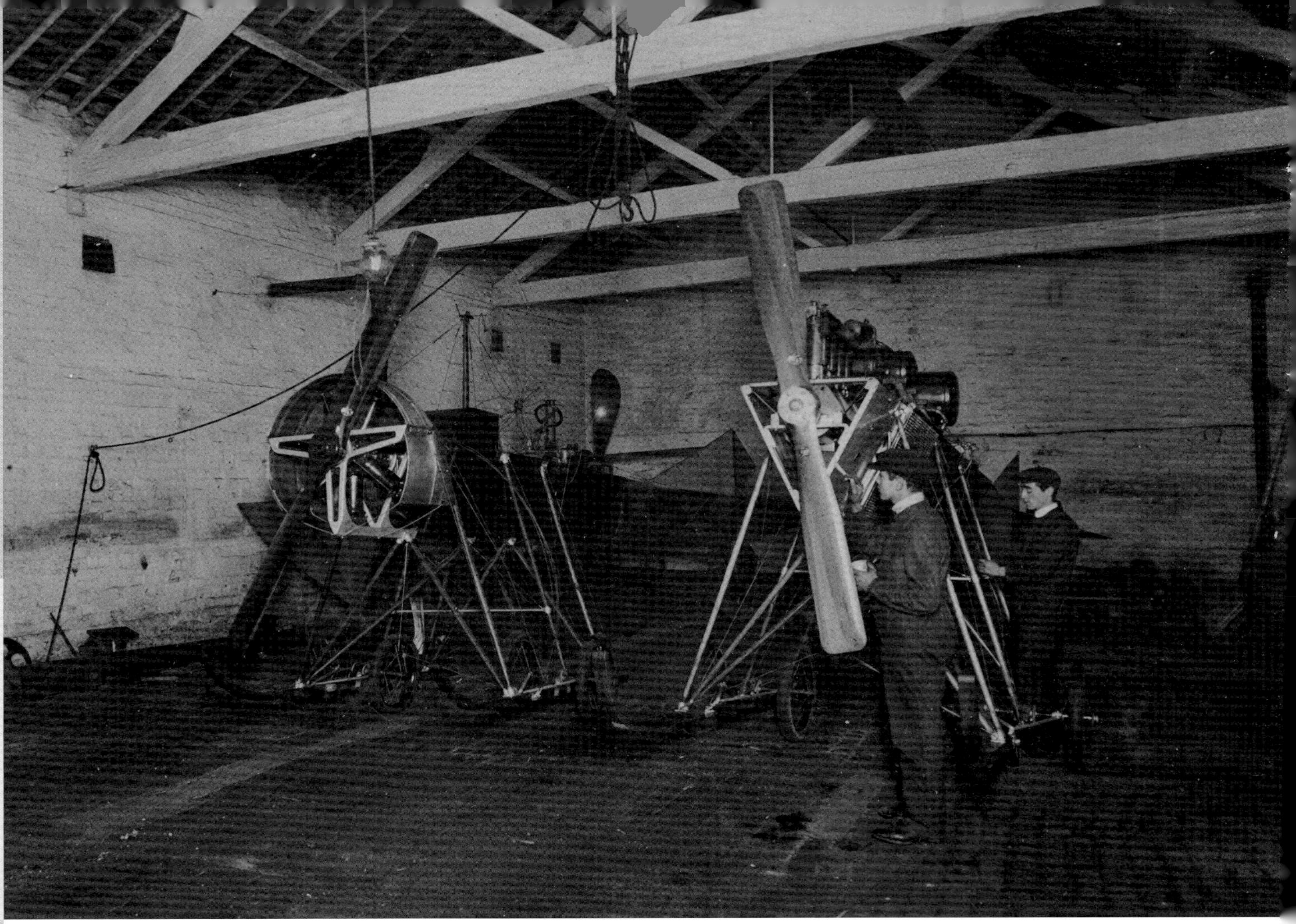

population of 625,000, almost all of them living in homes heated by coal, it also had thriving commercial, retail and industrial sectors, whose offices, shops and factories all relied on coal.

Bayford & Co, coal merchants, first appears in local trade directories in 1923, when it was based in Owen Chambers, 4, Duncan Street, Leeds. This was in the heart of the city; Duncan Street linked two of its main thoroughfares, Briggate and Boar Lane. Owen Chambers was home to several other businesses, including the Allied Artists Corporation Ltd; Mitchell N Gladstone & Co, safe makers; George E Nicholson, business transfer agent; George Richards, an iron merchant; Stanton & Smailes, surveyors; Daniel & Royle Ltd, paper agents; and the Leeds representative of the Kitson Engineering Company (London) Ltd. In 1925, the firm moved to 30, Park Cross Street, close to Park Square, and ten minutes' walk away from Duncan Street. Once again it was an address

shared with others, including a woollen manufacturer, solicitor and manufacturer's agent.

By 1929, the business was doing well enough to lease space at the London & North Eastern Railway Company's depot in South Accommodation Road, where trains transported coal directly from the collieries for distribution throughout the city. But this was the year of the Wall Street Crash, which heralded one of the worst global economic depressions, causing countless businesses to fail and throwing millions of people out of work around the world. By 1932, Bayford & Co had given up its city centre office, concentrating all its activities on South Accommodation Road.

By then, the business was under the daily direction of 26-year-old Fred Turner. For the next quarter of a century, he would remain in charge, winning the trust and respect of the founding partners.

1937-64

3

Fred Turner

Fred Turner spent his entire working life with Bayford & Co. He joined as an office boy in 1922 and retired as chairman in 1971, by which time he owned half the business. No one knows who ran Bayford in its earliest years but evidently the founders found Fred reliable and trustworthy. Within a few years he was running the business.

Fred built up the business in and around Leeds during the 1920s and 1930s. By the late 1930s, it was probably turning over around £2 million a year in today's values. Coal was delivered throughout the city, firstly by horse and cart, later by a small fleet of motor wagons, all based at South Accommodation Road. It was hard work, with men turning up at the yard at the crack of dawn to shovel coal from heaps into sacks, heaving them onto their carts before they set off on their deliveries to the terraced streets, housing estates, offices and factories scattered around the city. With their regular rounds, the coalmen got to know their customers well, developing a reputation for good timekeeping and customer service. Coalmen were trusted.

Leeds in the 1930s - Duncan Street and Boar Lane. (Leeds Library and Information Service, www.leodis.net)

Bayford and the Turner family

Bayford & Co has been managed by three successive generations of the Turner family. The Turners were a Leeds family, hailing from Armley, working in the boot and shoe trade and the textile industry. Born in 1906, Fred Turner joined the company as office boy and ended up owning half of it as managing director. He married Maud Webster in 1930 and they had three children: Peggy, born in 1931; David, born in 1938; and John, born in 1945. David joined the business in 1958, followed by John ten years later, and in 1972 they bought the company. David's sons Jonathan and Paul, and John's son Andrew all joined Bayford. Jonathan took over from his father as managing director in 2000 and four years later bought the business from his father and uncle. Today, Bayford & Co Ltd is only one part of Jonathan's extensive business interests, ranging from energy, property and hospitality to various charitable and other interests.

Fred and Maud Turner on their wedding day.

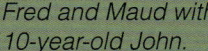

Fred and Maud with 10-year-old John.

Many customers kept their coal inside their houses, leaving keys to allow their coalmen to gain access, or leaving their doors unlocked. The coalman was just one of a series of trusted deliverymen. These were the days when people expected almost daily deliveries of all sorts, from bread, milk and eggs to coal.

The Limited Company

By 1937, the turnover of the business was large enough for the founders to decide that the time had come to convert the partnership into a limited company. As managing director, Fred was probably already a partner. He became the single largest shareholder in the new company, owning just under half of Bayford & Co Ltd when it was incorporated on 13 March 1937. The founders were winding down their participation in the business. Frank Baker substantially reduced his holding, and on 2 October 1939, one month after the declaration of war, William Chambers resigned from the board (he died in the following year). Benjamin Binks, on the other hand, continued to take an interest in the business, remaining as chairman almost continuously until his death in 1965.

By 1937, times were improving. The worst of the long depression, which had thrown so many

Fred Turner became the single largest shareholder in the new company

people out of work for so long, was over. Cheap money was funding a boom in new housing, which meant more business for the coal merchant. Industry too was reviving, aided by the government's rearmament programme. In the short time before war broke out again across Europe, Bayford prospered. At the annual general meeting on 27 September 1938, three days before Neville Chamberlain returned from meeting Hitler to declare he had achieved 'peace in our time', shareholders were full of praise for Fred Turner. Declaring a 20 per cent dividend, Fred told them Bayford had won more business for the sale of coke and had kept two wagons on the road.

Wartime

The war brought uncertainty for the business although the coal industry escaped heavy regulation, which helped firms such as Bayford to survive. Caution was Fred's watchword, and he was reported telling his fellow shareholders in 1940 that 'they must carry on as cautiously as possible until stable conditions returned'.

The Coal Industry in War and Peace

Bayford & Co managed to navigate the difficulties of doing business in wartime with some success. Some industries were heavily regulated from the outbreak of war and many businesses failed to survive. Coal, however, was never rationed although it was subject to regulation. But productivity suffered, since mining was not classed as a reserved occupation and many men had left for the forces. This was compounded by a shortage of raw materials, plant and equipment and poor industrial relations in the privately owned mines. To plug the labour gap, the government called up thousands of young men to work in the mines. These were the Bevin Boys, named after Ernest Bevin, the wartime minister of labour.

Although the industry was nationalised in 1946, coming under the management of the National Coal Board, this did little to solve its long-term problems. Industry began looking for other more reliable and cost-effective sources of energy, and domestic demand began to fall in the wake of clean air legislation to eliminate the deadly winter smogs.

The uncertainty surrounding the future of the industry was a fundamental reason why David Turner moved the business away from coal to oil. Although Bayford retained its coal interests until 1991, the UK industry steadily declined. Today not a single deep mine survives in the UK and coal provides just 2 per cent of the country's energy; in April 2017, the country experienced its first day without energy generated through fossil fuel since Thomas Edison opened the UK's first coal-fired power station in Holborn, London, in 1882.

Bayford trucks and drivers waiting to deliver coal.

Fred's step-sister Ethel came to work for the business when one of the office staff was called up for military service. She later recalled the small rented office in South Accommodation Road with its three rooms, one for a weighbridge, one for a general office and one for Fred Turner's office. The furniture and sanitary facilities were primitive (Fred's son John recalled that good advice was to make sure you had been to the toilet before you left for work) and there was no running hot water. During the winter or in wet weather, bags of coal were stacked near the fire to dry out. At a time of rationing, the firm had its own hand-wound petrol pump, with the handle under lock and key in the office.

Fred managed to expand business during the war. He took over another retail business, added more delivery rounds and increased the number of wagons in the fleet to five. He also began hiring out the wagons for general haulage at times of the year when there was less demand for coal. The chairman was full of praise for Fred's efforts in 1942, speaking 'in very high terms of the work performed during the years by Mr Turner, whose efforts had borne such satisfactory results'. By 1944/45, the company had sales of just over £64,000, equivalent to around £2.7 million in 2019.

Austerity

Fred extended his cautious wartime approach to the peacetime austerity that followed. There was no sudden return to national prosperity. In achieving victory, the country had crippled itself financially. Many wartime controls, including rationing, lasted well into the 1950s, while others, such as bread rationing, were introduced for the first time. Sweets were rationed until 1953, and meat until 1954. The state retained control over repairs and maintenance until 1948 and new building work until 1954. Basic materials, such as timber and steel, which were rationed, and bricks, which were not, were in short supply. By the end of the war, men and machinery were suffering from wear and tear after years of shortages. As Fred pointed out, 'The motor wagons were old and the men were very indifferent in the handling of the vehicles.' Productivity was low, standards having fallen through the wartime dilution of labour, whilst skilled men returning from active service were in need of retraining. On top of all this, the nationalisation of the coal industry created more uncertainty.

Then came one of the worst winters on record. Snow began falling heavily on 21 January 1947, temperatures plunged and the freezing conditions lasted until late March. Leeds

'The motor wagons were old and the men were very indifferent in the handling of the vehicles'

Corporation employed 16 snowploughs during the day and 36 every night. The pervading sense of national exhaustion was exemplified by the country's inability to produce enough power to meet demand, resulting in several months of power cuts as already struggling power stations became snowbound. Fred reported that 'during the winter the weather had rendered it difficult to clear sites and transport wood'. At South Accommodation Road, the handful of office staff shivered by the open fire that provided the only heat, while the absence of a kettle meant trudging through the snow to nearby Nellie's Transport Cafe to bring back mugs of tea.

Until wartime controls ended, merchants were fighting for scarce allocations and price-cutting was rife. Fred kept a close eye on costs and was always on the lookout to take over struggling smaller merchants to help increase the number of Bayford's customers. The company stayed in profit as sales increased, reaching £140,000 by 1954, with net profits of more than £3,700.

Coal in Decline

In that year the end of controls unleashed pent-up demand in the economy. As Harold MacMillan, the prime minister, famously remarked in 1957,

'You will see a state of prosperity such as we have never had in my lifetime – nor indeed in the history of this country. Indeed, let us be frank about it, most of our people have never had it so good.'

The challenge that faced Fred Turner was the steady decline in demand for coal from domestic and industrial consumers. Households

A Bayford Thames Trader truck with drivers in the late 1950s.

A Bayford tipper truck.

began moving away from coal in favour of cleaner fuels to heat their homes. For an increasing number of industrial, commercial and domestic users, their fuels of choice became oil

and gas, which were both much cheaper than they later became. To combat these changes, Fred not only continued to snap up customers from smaller merchants going out of business, but he also began seeking customers further afield in the county. By the late 1950s, Bayford had contracts with the National Coal Board to buy coal and coke from various depots and collieries for delivery to customers in Leeds, Bradford, Halifax, Huddersfield and many other parts of the West Riding of Yorkshire. Among them, for instance, was Lister & Co, whose Manningham Mills, with their majestic chimney, were an established Bradford landmark and a reminder of the days when coal was indeed king.

Nevertheless, the signs marking the steady decline of the coal industry were evident. For David Turner, Fred's 19-year-old son, it was obvious from the moment he joined the business in 1958 that the company needed to change direction. It was David's energy and vision that made sure Bayford continued to flourish as many more coal merchants shrank and shrivelled away.

1964-72

4

David Turner

When David Turner joined Bayford, he quickly came to two conclusions: firstly, that there was more profit from major industrial customers than from the many hundreds of domestic consumers; and, secondly, that concentrating on industrial users gave Bayford the opportunity to sell the oil that many of them were turning to. Oil was not only cheaper than coal, it also required much less work for the distributor. As David would remark later, 'We really went into the oil distribution business in a commercial way ... when the solid fuel business met with tremendous competition from other fuels.'

David's positive approach contrasted with the habitual caution of his father and they would clash constantly over the future of the business. One man was at the beginning of his business

David Turner's positive approach contrasted with the habitual caution of his father

career, the other coming towards the end; one man was ambitious for growth, the other conscious of preserving what he had built up.

The Oil Business

Moving into oil was a logical step for the business to take. Although Fred was anxious about investing in an area about which he knew nothing, his son was persistent. In 1963, David persuaded his father to let him discuss the idea with Total Oil Products (GB) Ltd, Total's UK subsidiary. In December 1964, Bayford announced that it had reached an agreement with Total for the distribution of oil products.

It was a propitious time to begin a new venture. Although the British economy had mixed fortunes during the 1960s, economic growth still averaged around 3 per cent a year. Bayford's oil distribution business began on 1 January 1965. David Turner had already ordered the company's first oil tanker (registration EWT544C) from John Caswell of Kenning Road Tankers. With the addition soon afterwards of a second small tanker, Bayford started transporting oil from Total's coastal refineries, storing it at a depot in Leeds and then distributing it to customers. The premises in South Accommodation Road were adapted for oil storage, leading the company to move to a new location nearby. In 1967, Bayford leased from the British Railways Board a modern office block and substantial yard in Pepper Road.

The first Bayford oil tanker supplied by John Kenning Road Tankers in 1965.

Pepper Road

For 20 years from 1967 to 1987 Pepper Road was the headquarters of Bayford & Co. Originally leased from the British Railways Board, it was a large site, with a purpose-built office block, a maintenance garage, and a yard for the fleet of lorries. Four staff worked in the small general office. The telephone switchboard was operated by Doreen Whitby until late afternoon when other staff took turns to answer incoming calls. When things were really busy, David Turner himself would vet the calls he wanted to take. David's mother, Maud, also helped out by working on the telephone switchboard, franking mail and making the morning tea. Ethel Dale made tea in the afternoon, her main job being the preparation of accounts on the Burroughs accounting machine, before the system was computerised in the early 1970s. Correspondence was prepared by a single part-time typist. Stationery was issued, with reluctance, by Fred Turner, who still handled all the banking and wages.

Things had changed by the time Julie O'Shaughnessy began working in the accounts office in December 1984. On the ground floor were accounts and IT, managing the big mainframe computer; the solid fuel and oil sales departments; and a small transport office, where Frank Taylor was manager. Upstairs were the credit control department, Bayford Mining, and the directors' offices. 'It was a brilliant atmosphere.'

There was a great team, Julie recalled, among them Marlene Mortimer, popularly known as Grandma or Auntie. 'She was like a mother to all the young girls in the office.' For Debbie Franklin, who joined as an office junior in 1986, Marlene 'was like Mum to everybody. She would go to Morrison's every lunchtime with a big, long order, usually for sweets, crisps and pop, and fetch it all back for us. I learned a lot from Marlene over the years. If you didn't feel well, she would look after you.' 'I have such fond memories of Pepper Road,' recalled Julie. 'Everybody there made you feel welcome; it was like a family.'

When David Hobson joined Bayford's transport office at Pepper Road in 1985, he found 'it was a really happy place to work'. Working alongside the drivers, said David, gave him 'a great grounding in life skills'. When David was working an early shift, he was usually the only member of staff there, 'surrounded by hairy-arsed drivers, some of them rough and ready; it was hugely entertaining. It really was great fun and I learned a lot from it.' Among those men he recalled were Frank Morrison and Harry Thorpe, the first two drivers ever taken on by David Turner, each of them serving with the company for more than 30 years.

Pepper Road, Leeds, was the Bayford head office for many years. This is the Bayford Coal office, with (left to right) Doreen Whitby, Dennis Shooter, Dick Gordon (rear) and Brian Griffiths.

The Coal Business

While David was starting up Bayford's exciting new oil business, he also wanted to make more money from the coal business, which was still a substantial part of Bayford's activities.

The company had steadily expanded its distribution of coal beyond the West Riding. Although Bayford was now delivering coal all over the UK, its strength lay in the north of England. Almost all the coal came from collieries in Yorkshire – the company's maxim, noted one newspaper article in 1969, was 'Where Yorkshire coal is required, we will deliver it' – and the company's many customers included factories, government departments, hospitals, local authorities, schools and steel works. Bayford also sold coal wholesale to other merchants with their own retail depots. David Turner made sure the company remained competitive by investing in up-to-date plant and equipment. In 1969, reported the same article, Bayford's depot in Balm Road, Leeds, was 'equipped with the latest in modern handling equipment. Coal arrives by the train load and is unloaded by mechanical grabs and shovels, and merchants load their vehicles from coal hoppers.' By 1972, Bayford was delivering 25,000 tons of coal weekly to power stations in Yorkshire and Lancashire. Coal was still the most important source of energy in the UK and

'Where Yorkshire coal is required, we will deliver it'

Bayford Glover

Like many SMEs, Bayford has often turned to joint ventures, with all their advantages and disadvantages, to fulfil its ambitions. It was David Turner who first adopted the joint venture in pursuit of growth. Bayford Glover, formed in 1969, was the earliest.

The aim of the new partnership was to win one of the CEGB's new combined contracts to supply coal to groups of power stations. Bayford's partner was another coal factoring business, Sidney Glover & Co Ltd, which had also been supplying individual power stations. The firm had been a near neighbour of Bayford's, using the same goods depot in Hunslet, just off South Accommodation Road. Together they formed Bayford Glover Ltd on 1 August 1969, with David Turner and John Glover as joint managing directors.

The new venture won an initial two-year contract worth £4 million annually to supply coal to the Wakefield A, Ferrybridge A and B power stations. Bayford Glover supplied coal from 15 collieries in the Wakefield–Castleford area. Bayford Glover, and following its demise, Bayford itself, retained the contract with the CEGB until 1986. Bayford Glover supplied 10,000 tons of coal weekly to power stations on Teesside as well as 50,000 tons of grey shale for the lagoons that collected the pulverised ash left over from burning coal.

the country's hundred or more coal-fired power stations depended on a ready supply of coal from around five hundred deep mines and around a hundred opencast mines.

David was always quick to spot new opportunities. One came along in the late 1960s. For some years Bayford had negotiated contracts with individual power stations for the supply of coal. Then the Central Electricity Generating Board (CEGB) decided that instead of putting out to tender contracts for single power stations, it would group stations together to create bigger contracts. David Turner's instinct towards new challenges was always positive. Rather than give up the work, he decided Bayford could not only retain but could also increase its business with the CEGB by teaming up with another partner. In 1969, this led to Bayford's first joint venture: Bayford Glover Ltd, which won the contract and retained it until 1986.

David Turner's entrepreneurial panache was transforming the business. Between 1959 and 1969 Bayford increased its turnover ten times, recording sales of more than £2.5 million in the latter year, equivalent in 2019 to £39 million. As the company grew, David put more senior managers in place, including a sales director, Cliff Peacock, appointed in 1966. What David also wanted was someone to look after the company's finances, though he waited until 1968 before making a decision. In that year his younger brother John, just 22 years old, qualified as a chartered accountant, joining his brother in the business. It was the beginning of a successful partnership that lasted nearly 40 years.

John Turner's calm demeanour and grasp of detail, evident even at a young age, was probably reassuring for his father, who had often been at cross-purposes with his oldest son. This probably reassured him when David pushed for Bayford to develop its own retail petrol brand. Fred might also have been persuaded by David's argument that he was only doing what Fred had done years before, trying to find business for the company's vehicle fleet during quieter times of the year. As David later remarked,

'We had a problem utilising our tankers. They were busy delivering oil in the autumn and winter and to find work for them in spring and summer we went into petrol.'

Petrol Retailing

The late 1960s was the high point of petrol retailing in terms of the number of forecourts in operation. Unlike today, most were small and most employed attendants to fill customers' cars. Supermarkets were only just beginning to sell petrol. The market was populated with operators large and small, all competing for custom to win the high volumes they needed to break even in a high-fixed-cost, low-margin business. But competition was rarely on price: forecourt promotions ranged from highlighting the quality of branded fuel, particularly its octane number, to giving away drinking glasses and offering stamps or gifts for each gallon of fuel purchased.

David Turner, on the other hand, chose to differentiate his new venture from his many competitors solely on price. When Bayford first

David and John Turner

David Turner left West Leeds High School without any qualifications at the age of 15. After leaving James Hare in 1958, he moved to Bayford & Co, where his first job was shovelling coal, carrying coal sacks on his back, and driving delivery lorries.

David was always ambitious. As soon as he joined, he was looking for ways to change the company for the better. His relationship with his father was not easy, but Fred accepted the need for Bayford to add new activities to its existing coal business, which led to the start of oil distribution in 1964.

It was to make sure relations between father and son stayed on an even keel that David's brother **John** joined Bayford in 1968. After leaving Leeds Grammar School, John qualified as a chartered accountant with the company's auditors in Leeds. He had only just qualified when he was asked to join his brother. 'I wasn't really destined for the family business,' recalled John, 'but it became clear in my final year as David and my father were falling out. David wanted to expand and father didn't, but they both seemed to agree they needed a financial pair of hands, and that's what brought me into the business.' Detail was never David's strong point and

he welcomed the attention to detail John brought to finance.

It was an ideal business partnership. The brothers complemented each other: David more entrepreneurial, more willing to take risks, better at the big picture than the details; John more cautious, more considered in taking decisions, more meticulous. John described their relationship as, 'I took on the role of holding my brother back. We knew each other's strengths and weaknesses and they blended. I was the financial man and David was the go-getting salesman.' They worked well together and shared everything equally, including ownership of the business when they bought it in 1972, the year after their father, Fred, retired from active management.

They were also the figureheads of the business, liked and respected as good employers who always took an interest in the people who worked for them. As David Hobson recalled, 'David and John always used to look out for me; they were smashing people to work for. They knew who you were; they had a presence about them; they were respected; they always had the time of day for you.'

began supplying petrol, under the brand name Thrust, it was selling at up to half a shilling less per gallon than its rivals when a gallon typically cost 6s 6d (equivalent to around £5 a gallon today in real terms). As Cliff Peacock, Bayford's sales director, later remarked, Bayford offered '… northerners what they want: an on-the-spot cash saving rather than stamps, tumblers or pictures of soccer stars'.

The Origins of Thrust

On 1 July 1969, Bayford launched its retail petrol business under the brand name Thrust. It was accompanied by a logo featuring an outline of Concorde, the aviation wonder of the age, and the inspiration for the brand name of David Turner's new venture.

The first commercial airliner capable of supersonic speeds, Concorde was an Anglo-French project. The French prototype flew for the first time from Toulouse on 2 March 1969, followed by the British prototype on 9 April 1969, piloted by Brian Trubshaw. On that day David Turner was listening to a news report of that historic first flight. He had already settled on a brand name – Punch – which he thought would strike customers as similar to other popular independent brands of the day, such as Power and Jet. Listening to the radio reporter describe Concorde's take-off, he changed his mind. The word that caught his imagination was 'thrust': 'It is a word,' David said later, 'that comes to mind with energy and movement.'

Thrust began with one pump on a forecourt in Ossett in the West Riding. Dick Gordon, Bayford's service-station manager, later recalled that 'few of the motorists who pulled in to fill their tanks with the low-priced petrol with a strange name at that pump in Ossett can have realised that they were in on the start of a new petrol empire'.

David Turner later reflected on the challenges he had faced. 'Here was a local oil and coal distributor entering a market completely dominated by the international oil companies who controlled the flow of petroleum products into the United Kingdom and marketed most of the petrol sold in the country through their own company-owned sites. How would they react to a newcomer? Most important of all, how would the customers react? Seven years ago, one was lucky to get a tiger's tail, a pair of tights or a glass in return for the numerous coupons one had collected from the petrol supplier. Here was Thrust offering 6d a gallon off the price! The motorists soon began to realise they had had enough of tails, tights and glasses and would prefer to have a cash saving.'

The Thrust logo, with the influence of Concorde clearly visible..

Joanne Pease, a Bayford PA, filling up at a Thrust service station.

A Bayford tanker in Thrust livery in 1972.

David Turner's ambition was not to create a network of wholly owned filling stations; the company didn't have the money for such an ambitious strategy. Instead, he aimed to sign up existing independent retailers, particularly those in more remote or rural locations, where major oil companies supplied petrol at a premium. It wasn't easy to make inroads in a competitive market, especially once the supermarkets began to expand their own retail fuel operations. Nevertheless, although Thrust remained a minor player, by 1972 the brand was selling 10 million gallons of fuel every year, almost all of it supplied by Total from its refinery on the Lincolnshire coast. Bayford began building up a

small portfolio of its own sites, either leased or purchased, and started to venture into marketing, promoting the brand through flyers, leaflets and newspaper advertising.

By 1972, thanks to its oil distribution and retail petrol activities, as well as its solid fuel business, Bayford's turnover had increased to £8 million, three times greater than in 1969, while net profits had risen over the same period from £18,000 to more than £200,000. As one newspaper reported, within the business there was 'a definite atmosphere of being ready to tackle almost anything in its own field or associated ones'.

1972-88

5

Running this fast-growing organisation, David and John Turner were still young men: David in his early thirties, John in his late twenties. The business was completely different from the one David had joined, not only bigger, but also more entrepreneurial, more ambitious. Fred was no longer actively involved. Yet, while the brothers were solely responsible for the fortunes of the company, they had no stake in it. Their father still owned half the shares while the remainder was in the hands of the families of the founders, who were even more remote from the business.

Buying the Business

The brothers decided they had to control their own destiny. Fred was happy to sell them his half of the business and he advised his sons on how to approach the other shareholders. David and John never had any doubts that they were doing the right thing. Each of them borrowed £18,000, worth around £250,000 in 2019, to finance the purchase. The company's bankers, Barclays, were willing to make the loan without any security other than the shares. The brothers repaid their debts at £400 every quarter. In 1972, the ownership of the business passed from one generation to another.

The brothers decided they had to control their own destiny

It was a brave decision made at a time when the British economy was deteriorating rapidly. The era of cheap oil was coming to an end. A serious energy crisis erupted in 1973, when the major oil-supplying countries, members of the Organisation of Petroleum Exporting Countries, cut back production. Prices rocketed, with the cost of a barrel of oil tripling within a year.

Diversification

When David Turner set out to create an integrated energy business, he began by trying to bolt new businesses onto Bayford's existing activities, with varying degrees of success.

There was an abortive attempt to exploit onshore and offshore oil deposits with other partners through a subsidiary, which became Bayford Exploration in 1979. Instead, five years later, changing its name to Bayford Mining, the business switched its focus to the development of opencast mining as the closure of the country's deep mines accelerated. This too was ultimately unsuccessful and unprofitable. John Turner remembered David visiting an opencast site in Scotland. 'He took a handful of coins out of his pocket and threw them into the quarry as if to say it was money down the drain. He'd gone off the idea by then!'

More successful were plans to augment the company's transportation and storage operations. To reduce reliance on road transport, Bayford invested in the infrastructure to bring oil up inland waterways from coastal refineries. Fleet Storage Co Ltd was formed in 1974 as a joint venture with

David Turner had a vision of an integrated energy business

Bayford Exploration trucks in action.

Bayford's transport workshop in Lotherton Way, Leeds. (Centre)

another oil distributor, Shaw's Fuels Ltd. The company took over an existing disused oil storage depot on the banks of the Aire and Calder Navigation at Woodlesford on the outskirts of Leeds. This became an important part of the business, freeing Bayford from reliance on third parties, giving it greater control over storage and distribution and cutting back the need for road transport. In 1993, Bayford became outright owners of the company.

In 1976, the joint venture partners teamed up with John H Whitaker (Tankers) Ltd to create Whitfleet Ltd, which owned and operated motor barges. Although Bayford continued to operate barges into the late 1990s, it was not a consistently profitable business.

There were a number of other minor joint ventures that varied in their success. The drawback of all the time and investment expended on David Turner's vision was that it hindered the more rapid expansion of Bayford's core fuel-retailing and distribution businesses and gave an opportunity to rivals entering the same markets. This was apparent by the early 1980s and David Turner began to regret his enthusiasm for joint ventures, commenting in the wake of one failure that 'we should never again get involved in a situation where we do not have control'.

Fleet Storage was formed in 1974 at the Woodlesford site on the Aire & Calder Navigation, supplied with fuel by barge from coastal refineries.

Named after Betty Whitaker and Jean Turner, the Betty-Jean was a general purpose cargo vessel launched in 1985.

The price of petrol rose so sharply that there was even talk in the UK of a return to petrol coupons. It took the British economy more than a decade to recover.

As the oil crisis was placing a question mark over the future of Thrust, the coal industry was also in trouble. There were two bitter strikes in the early 1970s, which contributed to the defeat of the Conservative government in 1974. Bayford strove hard to make sure customers continued to receive the fuel they needed. When one Leeds factory threatened with strike action contacted the company to say it was running short of oil, a delivery was made within 20 minutes. The manager of Bayford's coal department, Peter Brayshay, recorded in the same year how

'our dealers and ourselves kept many thousands of homes warm during the power strike and miners' strike earlier this year. We delivered from our stocks when most of the merchants had no fuel. I am sure, once again, that our customers have confidence in our *ability to look after them during the forthcoming winter with its threatened power cuts.'*

Ten years later, the industry endured an even more damaging dispute, which was followed by a raft of pit closures, heralding the final decline of the UK industry.

Publicly, David Turner was always bullish about the future of coal; privately, he was more anxious. Building upon the oil distribution and fuel retail businesses, he had a vision of an integrated energy business, covering everything from coal mining and oil drilling to the barges, using inland waterways to bring fuel from coastal refineries. Bayford spent a decade trying to fulfil this vision, ultimately at the expense of the company's core activities.

Property

Other than the oil storage depot developed at Woodlesford, the most enduring example of the company's diversification strategy was its

David and John Turner with Terry Milner from the Variety Club, at the presentation by the company of a Variety Club of Great Britain Sunshine mini-bus for St Bernardette's School, Pudsey, in 1975.

KINDLY DONATED BY
BAYFORD OILS.
LEEDS 10

property business. The idea arose from a discussion between David Turner and one of his oldest friends, property developer Don Fryer. In 1977, they set up Bayford & Co (Developments) Ltd together, with Don owning 40 per cent of the business. The company built up a small portfolio of investment properties in and around Leeds, including flats, offices and shops. It also carried out a handful of developments, such as the office block completed in York Road, Seacroft, Leeds in 1983. Called Deacon House, it took its name from Fred Turner's father, whose name has been handed down through every successive generation of the family.

Fred Turner joined Bayford & Co at the age of 16 in 1922 as an office boy. When he died in 1984, he was chairman of the company, which he had passed on to his sons David and John.

Fibrelite and Aquasentry

Two of Bayford's investments were ventures outside the business, local enterprises with commercial potential just getting off the ground and looking for external capital.

The most successful was Fibresec, founded in Otley in 1980. Fibresec's great idea was a lightweight composite access cover, 60 per cent lighter than the traditional cover. For Bayford, this was an attractive investment. The most frequently lifted access covers were on filling-station forecourts, and tanker drivers were always complaining how heavy they were. Bayford provided the funds to begin making the new covers, which were marketed under the Fibrelite name. They were an instant success and quickly adopted by major oil companies in the UK. They also found an international market. Bayford, for instance, helped to introduce the cover to the USA, thanks to Marketing Director Ken Gardiner, who took a sample with him on a business trip.

The company changed its name to Fibrelite in 1993 and began developing similar products. 'This was probably our best diversification,' reflected John

Turner. Bayford eventually sold its stake, and in 2013 Fibrelite became a subsidiary of OPW, part of the US Dover Corporation, and in 2017 it reported sales of more than £12 million and profits of more than £3 million.

Bayford's second investment was in a firm called Aqualarm in 1988. Peter Docherty founded the business to develop water-detecting sensors for a local electricity company that had lost one of its transformers as a result of flooding. The sensor was launched commercially under the Aqualarm name in 1988 and it created a lot of interest in the UK and overseas. One device, for instance, was installed in London's Guildhall to protect one of the precious copies of the Magna Carta. Financially, however, the business struggled. For a time, Bayford partnered the investment company 3i in the business but Bayford became sole owners after buying out 3i's stake in 1999. In 2012, Bayford sold the company, by then called Aquasentry, to Rob Staines, who had been running it for the previous three years. In turn he sold the business to a competitor in 2016.

Oil, Petrol and Coal

From the early 1980s, Bayford concentrated on developing its oil distribution and fuel retail activities while planning the disposal of its solid-fuel business. After the miners' strike of 1984, the writing was on the wall for the UK coal industry. This was obvious to Ken Gardiner, who joined the company in 1985 with responsibility for the solid-fuel operation. Ken also recognised there was little future in Bayford's opencast mining activities. The disposal of the coal business was just a matter of time, so Ken used his contacts in the industry to find a suitable buyer. On 1 July 1991, Bayford Coal was sold to Anglo Coal, the culmination of a trend David Turner had spotted 30 years earlier. It marked the end of an involvement with solid fuels that had begun with the foundation of the business after the First World War.

By the mid-1980s, Bayford Oil was supplying everything from fuel for domestic customers to specialised lubricants for an aero industry firm in Yorkshire, ship bunker fuel for freighters working out of Humber and Lincolnshire ports, and fuel for all the US Defense Department's vessels stationed in the UK. To serve this widely varied customer base, Bayford maintained a mix of tankers in its transport fleet. Smaller tankers were ideal for the small rural petrol retailer or the smallest domestic customer. 'Our small tankers,' said Transport Manager Frank Taylor in 1979, 'are ideal for delivering to farms, shops and houses. No delivery is too small for us.'

As for Thrust, by 1983 the brand could be found on 200 forecourts in Yorkshire, Lincolnshire, Nottinghamshire, Derbyshire, Lancashire, Cheshire and North

> *The disposal of the coal business was just a matter of time*

A typical Bayford Thrust retail petrol station.

Wales. But the brand was still in the minor league and competition was becoming more acute as the supermarkets expanded their fuel retailing operations. The days when Thrust led the way in price discounting had long since gone; the cheaper prices once unique to Thrust were now on offer from many other suppliers.

David Turner with his outgoing character and entrepreneurial flair had become something of a pin-up boy for regional entrepreneurs. In 1983, Bayford was listed as 65th among Britain's top 100 private companies. In 1984, one journalist wrote, 'It is no secret that David Turner aims to make Bayford one of the top 50 private companies, having already steered them to their position of Britain's largest private fuel company. He and his young management team look set to achieve that ambition in the near future.' In the following year, David was profiled by the The Yorkshire Post's industrial correspondent, Robin Morgan. 'It would not be hard to picture Mr David Turner as the central character in a glossy television soap series.' Yet Bayford's turnover and profits peaked in the mid-1980s. It would take the company almost a decade before it exceeded the turnover of nearly £70 million achieved in 1985, while net profits of more than £1.4 million recorded in 1984 would not be surpassed until 2006.

For several years Bayford sponsored the talented English golfer Howard Clark, seen here with the Ryder Cup at the Bayford Golf Day in 1985, with David, Jonathan and John Turner.

David Turner at his desk in Pepper Road in the 1970s.

The Bayford management team in the late 1980s, with (left to right around the table) Keith Watson, Derrick Teed, Malcolm Jessop, Christopher Dean, Keith Grainger, Peter Haw, Lorraine Lowe, David Turner, John Turner, Ken Gardiner, Eunice Long, Sam Jackson and Martin Platt.

A Chance Encounter

David Turner was well known for being well dressed. David Hobson, Bayford's transport manager, had cause never to forget this. The transport section relocated to Fleet Storage's premises in Woodlesford in 1988. It was not a universally appreciated move. As David Hobson recalled, 'They promised us an office and they gave us a Portakabin: we had to pull the desks away from the windows when it rained to stop them getting wet.' The offices were freezing in winter and stifling in summer. During a warm spell in the summer of 1988, David and his colleagues dressed accordingly. One afternoon David had just returned

to the offices after washing his new company car. 'I'd just come back from the shower, down to my Scooby-Doo T-shirt and checked shorts, and Sam [Jackson] was still there in his deckchair, when DDT [David Turner] arrived.' It caught everyone by surprise for such visits were rare. The timing, recalled David, could not have been more embarrassing. 'He was in his blue pin-striped suit, his blue shirt with his white collar, a really smart tie, and he had his jacket on, not a bead of sweat on him, looking immaculate. He had fun with that incident many times, often ringing down and saying, "I hope you're a bit more suitably attired today, David."'

1988-99

6

In January 1988, Bayford moved out of its offices in Pepper Road after more than 20 years. The company's new home was Bowcliffe Hall, a listed Georgian mansion near the village of Bramham on the edge of the A1.

For some people, the journey to Bayford's new head office was too long and they left the company. For those who stayed, the company organised a bus to bring them to work. Ninety people were soon working from the Hall. At the same time, the company's transport operations were relocated to Lotherton Way, Leeds, and to Fleet Storage Co's Woodlesford site.

As Bayford's newsletter put it, 'The move from Pepper Road to Bowcliffe Hall has, without a

'The move has, without a doubt, put increased vigour into all of us.'

doubt, put increased vigour into all of us.' 'It was quite a change,' confirmed Debbie Franklin. 'We'd gone from a fairly modern office to this big, vast building, with tennis court and pitch-and-putt in the grounds.' In fact, not only did the Hall possess tennis courts and pitch-and-putt, it also had its own cricket pitch with a pavilion that was widely loved in the cricketing world. There were 20 acres of formal gardens, employing two gardeners and an apprentice. Accounts and IT were located in the partitioned former ballroom; the sales team worked from rooms to the right of the main entrance; and the solid fuel division was housed in the Hall's west wing. The catering was excellent. 'What tempted us,' recalled Julie O'Shaughnessy, 'was the two-course meal.'

Bayford acquired Bowcliffe Hall in late 1987.

Bowcliffe Hall

The opportunity for Bayford to buy Bowcliffe Hall came when Hargreaves was taken over by the Coalite Group in 1986. The idea came from Ken Gardiner, who had once worked for Hargreaves at Bowcliffe Hall. David and John Turner agreed with him; they could all see that the Hall had potential for a number of uses as well as providing Bayford with a new headquarters. Towards the end of 1987 Bayford bought the property for £955,000.

Bowcliffe Hall is a magnificent Georgian mansion. The building of it commenced in 1805 by William Robinson, a wealthy cotton spinner from Manchester, but he completed only the west wing before he was declared bankrupt. The property was sold to Joan Smyth, who was in residence by 1822 and completed the Hall some three years later. After his death in 1840, the house was sold to the Lane Fox family from neighbouring Bramham Park who altered and extended the property. In 1907, it was sold again to another businessman: Walter Jackson, who was the chairman and managing director of the mining company, Henry Briggs, Son & Company. The company was the largest coal producer in the West Yorkshire coalfields, owning Whitwood Collieries near Normanton in the West Riding until nationalisation in 1946.

In 1917, the house became the home of its most distinguished owner. The achievements of aviation pioneer Robert Blackburn would inspire the later development of the property under Jonathan Turner. Percy Kitchen began working there in 1950. 'My mother was cook and my sister was a housemaid for Mr Blackburn, and I became his manservant when I was demobbed from the RAF in 1950. ... When we worked for Mr Blackburn, we were part of the family. There was an air of gentility about the place.' Percy remembered famous names from the heyday of the British aircraft industry visiting Robert Blackburn, including Sir Geoffrey de Havilland, Sir Thomas Sopwith and Sir Frederick Handley Page.

The house ceased to be a home after Blackburn's death in 1955 although he had already moved to Devon to live in semi-retirement two years previously. This time the Hall was sold to the Hargreaves Group, another coal business, for use as their headquarters. The Group's chairman, Brigadier Kenneth Hargreaves, a decorated soldier as well as an industrialist, was the last Lord Lieutenant of the West Riding and the first of West Yorkshire, a link with the Lieutenancy continued today by Jonathan Turner as one of West Yorkshire's Deputy Lieutenants. Joan Buchanan remembered the strict regime under Brigadier Hargreaves. Staff had to cross from one wing to another not by the main hall but through the cellar. Men had to keep their jackets on and women were forbidden to wear trousers. Depending on status, people dined either in the canteen, the mess for senior managers and junior directors, or the dining room for the main board.

Bayford Energy tankers provide the foreground to Bowcliffe Hall soon after it became Bayford's new head office in 1988.

Every Friday, for example, fish and chips was followed by sticky toffee pudding. 'John Turner,' remarked Sally Genn, 'said he could watch people's waistlines increasing!' In addition, a tea trolley came round the offices every morning and afternoon, sometimes laden with leftovers from functions.

Although the Hall was impressive externally, internally it was tired. Maintenance had been neglected as frequent leaks testified, although the property as a whole was structurally sound. For Mark Kilvington, who joined Bayford in 1991, the Hall 'was never quite as grand as people made it out to be and it was never the place to run an oil business from'. From time to time, when the company was not performing as well, questions were even asked about whether the Hall was too great a burden. The idea of selling it was always turned down but it was only many years later that funds became available to transform the Hall's interior and grounds.

One of the property's advantages was its potential for commercial letting. The old stable block was redeveloped into offices, the left-hand side as Bowcliffe Court, the right-hand side as Bowcliffe Grange, completed within two years of Bayford buying the Hall. When the west wing became available, that too was let. The first commercial tenant in the Hall itself was Victor Watson, the former chairman of Waddington's, who took over Ken Gardiner's office after Ken retired in 1995.

Hospitality was another opportunity. First, lunches were held in the main dining room. Then, in September 1991, the Hall hosted its first wedding reception. The lawn was used for marquees and the dining room for drinks. Three years later, the Marriage Act permitted weddings to take place for the first time on approved premises other than a register office. On 15 July 1995, the Hall hosted the wedding of John Turner's daughter Jayne to Richard Groom. One of the attractions of the grounds was an ancient chapel of ease built by the monks of Nostell Priory. Although it was not licensed for weddings, it was available for services of blessing. The first couple to have their marriage blessed were Richard and Nicola Woods in the spring of 1993, supported by 25 guests who squeezed into the chapel.

Jonathan Turner and Liz Slater: Changing Culture

The partnership between Jonathan Turner and Liz Slater transformed Bayford. They both joined the company in the same year, 1988, and soon became friends.

Liz Slater grew up in South Africa, where she studied at Natal University, graduating in industrial psychology and sociology. She came to the UK looking for work when she was 22. Before joining Bayford, she took a post-graduate qualification in management from Leeds Metropolitan University. She was interviewed by Ken Gardiner. 'I remember sitting in the room and Liz came in and I thought even if she's not right for this job, we need her because she impressed me with how absolutely straight and honest she was. Within weeks, we could see we were right.' The decision to appoint her, said Jonathan, 'changed my life, John's life, my father's life, because ultimately what happened was that our paths became closer and closer, and she became a co-conspirator: how she felt the business should be was how I felt the business should be, so we spent a lot of time changing things from within, sort of with my father's blessing, because he wasn't really interested in the detail'.

Jonathan graduated in management and marketing from Newcastle Polytechnic. He couldn't understand why so many of his peers were uninterested in running their own businesses. He read widely on business, devouring books by tycoons of the time, such as James Hanson, James Goldsmith and Nigel Broakes. He always wanted to join Bayford but he was determined to make his own mark. 'I wanted to be my own person.' This determination to achieve things on his own terms would remain one of Jonathan's strongest characteristics. He hated being known as David Turner's son; he knew had a lot to live up to, because his father was himself a charismatic and widely respected businessman. 'It was challenging being David Turner's son, trying to be yourself, trying to make your own success.' Jonathan was soon convinced that the business was ready for change. He felt the family firm had become 'an old, mature, slightly sleepy business. It wasn't run in any aggressive, motivational manner, and people were ready to leave at five.'

From early on it was clear that they complemented each other's skills, Jonathan brimming over with ideas, Liz adept at implementing them. They soon began sharing their views about the future of the business. While they both became inspirational team leaders, it was Jonathan who relished meeting people, developing contacts and standing up in public while Liz was never much interested either in networking or publicity.

Jonathan Turner was 'a young man with lots of confidence'

Jonathan Turner and Liz Slater

In the same year that Bayford took over Bowcliffe Hall, two young people joined the company whose influence on the business in the long term would be immense. The first, in June, was Elizabeth Hill, later better known to everyone as Liz Slater; the second, in September, was Jonathan Turner, David Turner's eldest son.

Liz in 1988 found Bayford to be 'a very traditional business, and the guys who ran the business were true gentlemen'. She received encouragement from Ken Gardiner, the marketing director; Martin Platt, who later became commercial director; and Keith Watson, the company secretary. Liz began by selling oil over the telephone before widening her experience in other parts of the business and becoming sales manager for Bayford Oil in 1993. As she remembered,

'I was totally allowed to do my own thing. I was given a huge amount of opportunity, a huge amount of flexibility, and I cannot ever recall anyone ever saying I couldn't do something. Everybody was totally, totally supportive. We had the run of the place.'

Jonathan started by selling coal. He was, said Ken Gardiner, 'a young man with lots of confidence'. Sent to manage the Northallerton oil depot in 1990, he was astonished to be told that he was making too many sales calls every day, and he soon began pushing for change.

Father and son: David and Jonathan Turner.

A young Liz Slater with the ISO9002 award, with senior management: (left to right) David Travis (Thrust), David Savage (Northallerton oil depot), Derrick Teed (Bayford Electronics), Martin Platt (commercial director), Liz Slater, Peter Haw (Bayford Oil), Tony Wragg (fleet engineer) and David Turner.

John Turner, Keith Watson, Ken Gardiner and David Turner in the hall at Bowcliffe Hall.

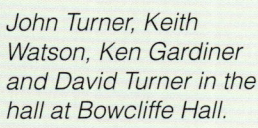

Liz and Jonathan soon became friends. They soon began comparing their experiences of the oil business and discussing how it could benefit from change. It was not so much that the business had stopped growing – in the early 1990s, under the continued leadership of David and John Turner, several acquisitions were made, including Holderness Fuel Supplies (1991) and Keighley Fuel Services (1993), and Bayford had set up outposts in North Wales and Norfolk – but it had the potential to grow more rapidly. For Jonathan and Liz, the key was changing the culture of the business. Credit controllers had more sway than the sales team. At one point fewer people were employed in sales than in the accounts and credit control departments. 'We had some credit managers who used to think they were God,' recalled Liz, 'and you used to have almost to beg to get orders to do your job in sales.' Jonathan remembered a visit to the company from Conoco's chief credit officer: it was a revelation to hear him say that he was there to work out how Conoco could sell more fuel to Bayford. 'Here was a credit controller acting as a salesman and saying to us how can we sell more together.' The business had to be driven by sales and marketing. If it wanted to beat the competition, reflected Jonathan, it could no longer be

The key was changing the culture of the business

'a very mature, nice-to-work-for family business, full of lovely long-serving people pottering around, operating in sectors that were dramatically changing. The business was fundamentally in the

'We really did start to have more fun'

Respect For Drivers

At the Northallerton oil depot, Jonathan soon learned how important it was to understand the business he was managing. Fed up with drivers telling him some deliveries were just too difficult to make, he decided he would learn to drive an HGV himself. Without telling anyone, he took lessons at the local HGV driving school, where he gained his Class I HGV licence. When he was told yet again that it was too unsafe to make a certain delivery, he decided he would deliver the oil himself. 'I went out into the yard, filled the tanker, with everyone watching, got into the tanker and drove off. But [the driver] was right – I couldn't do it either!' When Jonathan reached his destination, he found it was too hazardous to attempt to fill a precariously placed oil tank in imminent danger of collapsing and causing contamination. He started to respect the drivers' accumulated knowledge and expertise. 'But I got huge street "cred" from all the drivers in Bayford, and that was another part of my education, where I learned that when you have a certain role or position you have to have the ability to talk to absolutely everybody.'

Northallerton oil depot where Jonathan Turner gained managerial experience.

right sectors but the people were in the wrong place or the wrong age, and Liz and I thought we had to change the culture in the business.'

Able, enthusiastic, younger people were recruited to the more productive telesales team while the traditional field-based sales team was cut back. Newcomers included Mark Kilvington, who joined Bayford as a marketing assistant in 1991, and Chris Ritchie, who joined the telesales team in 1995. Methods of working became more professional, improving communications and service for customers. It was an almost immediate success. By the end of 1995, when June Forsyth was appointed as assistant sales manager to head up the new telesales team, 12 additional sales support staff had already been taken on. Under Mark Kilvington as group marketing manager, Bayford became one of the first oil distributors to adopt direct mail. The

Mark Kilvington joined Bayford in 1991.

technology was limited at the time, so every mailshot sent out had to be individually signed, folded and stuffed into envelopes; even Jonathan helped out from time to time. The company was also one of the first to use leaflet drops through the Royal Mail. A new generation of depot managers became more autonomous and therefore more accountable, with responsibility for everything from credit management to transport. 'We took down all the barriers,' said Liz, 'and let these guys run their own mini-businesses and that really worked.' The other thing that worked was encouraging people to enjoy their jobs. Both Liz and Jonathan believed people would work more productively if they had fun doing it. 'We really did start to have more fun,' said Liz. 'We had a lot of laughs in those days. At Christmas we used to sing carols to the customers and play a lot of very, very childish games.'

Chris Ritchie joined Bayford in 1995.

A Bayford Energy tanker making a domestic delivery, in this case, to the Leeds home of David Turner.

The Burmah Deal

As well as encouraging organic growth through a more positive sales-led culture, Jonathan was always on the lookout for potential acquisitions. He was always thinking bigger. His first major acquisition was also the biggest Bayford had ever carried out. The country's biggest independent filling-station operator, Frost Group (later Save Group), had recently taken over Burmah Castrol's fuel wholesale and retail business in the UK. David Turner knew James Frost since Bayford had sold him a handful of filling stations a year previously. David correctly calculated that James Frost would want to sell the oil distribution business. Jonathan led the negotiations that turned Bayford into the UK's largest privately-owned commercial oil distributor. For Jonathan, it was the chance he wanted to move out of his father's shadow and become known for what he did rather than for who he was.

The Burmah business was turning over £120 million a year, had 10,000 customers and for the first time gave Bayford a foothold in London and Scotland. Unprofitable parts of the business were sold off and others merged into Bayford's existing operations.

Fuel Cards

Thanks to Jonathan, Bayford seized another opportunity out of the Burmah deal. Since 1993, Bayford had started selling its own fuel cards after Jonathan had paid a visit out of curiosity to the pioneers of fuel cards in the UK, C H Jones, based in Walsall. By the time Jonathan was negotiating the purchase of the Burmah oil business, he was beginning to understand the profitable potential of fuel cards. As he later recalled,

'It was so easy. We could save the customers money and we could make lots of money without running all the petrol stations. We were selling, but it was somebody else's assets; somebody else was doing the deliveries of the fuel to somebody else's petrol station; and all I had to do was sell somebody's sales reps some fuel at below retail and the rest of it just happened.'

During the negotiations Jonathan realised that Frost's deal with Burmah Castrol also included a fuel-card business, operated on the Key Fuels bunkering network. Jonathan knew that Frost would have little interest in holding on to it, so he suggested to his colleagues that Bayford should buy it. This ran up against the prevailing negative attitude within the company, and the idea was rejected by Bayford's credit manager and accountant because it was too risky and involved too much administration. 'If I'd been a negative person,' said Jonathan, 'I would have said, yes, OK, but I was a positive person, and said to them, "We're just doing it".' He also had the support of his father and uncle. Within three years the expanded fuel-card business was proving consistently profitable.

As well as the oil distribution business, Thrust was growing but it was still small. Although it was selling only 20 million gallons of fuel every year in 1988, it was becoming more ambitious. In 1994, Bayford took over a number of filling stations from Elf, consolidating its position in Yorkshire, and from Texaco, extending its coverage in the north-east. In that year Bayford's sales exceeded £70 million while profits were more than £800,000.

The Business Under Pressure

All this optimism would soon disappear. The reason was the most sustained period of price-cutting the industry had ever seen. The major oil companies were facing growing competition from the increasing number of supermarket forecourts selling cheaper fuel. By the mid-1990s, the supermarkets had a fifth of the retail fuel market in the UK. The fight-back was led by Esso. In 1996, Esso launched its Price Watch campaign, cutting pump prices dramatically overnight.

Esso Price Watch

The price war precipitated by Esso's Price Watch campaign had what Jonathan Turner called a 'seismic' impact on the independent sector. Within a year, price cutting had cost the retail sector £1.2 billion, causing the closure of 1,500 forecourts, including 13 per cent of all privately owned sites, and the merger of several significant operators. It did nothing to lessen competition from the supermarkets. As for Bayford, said Jonathan Turner, 'what it immediately did to us was remove straightaway any profitability in the petrol retail business. But more importantly it hammered the balance sheet value of our assets.' With falling prices and fewer sales as customers turned to operators offering cheaper fuel, cashflow plummeted, leaving the entire business cash-strapped. 'I won't say we were in critical care,' said Liz Slater, 'but we were certainly in accident and emergency, waiting for someone to give a critical diagnosis.'

The Gator

The Gator was Bayford's imaginative way of raising Thrust's profile as price competition increased in the wake of the Esso Price Watch campaign. The jolly green and yellow giant rubber alligator was born in the spring of 1996 to launch Bayford's new points promotion, the 'Gatorway to Gifts'. The promotion was one of the first collect-points-for-prizes promotions and came with a magnetic-striped card for adding points.

It was, said one industry journal, 'the cheeriest promotion around, bringing back some jollity to our business'. The costume, with a huge moulded head, cost around a thousand pounds. The idea had been dreamed up by Nick Genn, Sally Genn's husband, whose logic was, if Esso could have a Tiger – the long-lived 'Put a Tiger in Your Tank' campaign had been hugely popular during the 1960s and 1970s – then why couldn't Bayford have a Gator? Not everyone was enthused by the idea, Jonathan Turner later remembered, but as he told his colleagues at the time, 'Hang on a minute; everybody in the industry has got their chin on the floor and there's a lot of shit flying around and maybe we should liven things up a bit.'

The Gator turned up in public for the first time to start the balloon race at the Markington Gala, near Ripon, on 27 May 1996 – two young children couldn't bear to be parted from him all afternoon. Employees took turns to dress up as the Gator, who appeared at a variety of locations, from petrol stations to schools. At the start of the autumn term in 1997, for instance, Gator turned up, with Jonathan Turner inside, to present a cheque at Monk Fryston junior school, where parents had been collecting points to raise funds. When all the children clambered onto the Gator's extensive tail, he began roaring loudly, which led them to chase him all around the playground. One child told him he couldn't possibly be a real Gator since he could see his socks.

The Gator.

The serious impact this had on Bayford, particularly on the value of its filling stations, caused the company's bank some concern. When several fuel suppliers made adverse changes to their credit terms, Bayford's borrowing requirements shot up by half. The bank asked accountants KPMG to carry out a review of the business. This was led by KPMG's corporate finance partner, Tony Sharp, who would later become a trusted advisor to Jonathan Turner. At the time, however, Jonathan hated the intrusion made by Tony and his team, although the review concluded that the business was sound, there was little risk to the bank, and the company's assets were more than sufficient as security. Nevertheless, all this reinforced the growing caution of David and John Turner.

Jonathan Turner was taking a more positive view. The business plan drawn up for the Bayford board in 1996 was called 'Continuing Entrepreneurial Direction'. It emphasised continued independence, strong leadership and a creative attitude towards new business and it highlighted the importance of an entrepreneurial board able to act flexibly and speedily to seize opportunities as they arose. There was a sense that more work was needed in order to reinvigorate the culture of the business and create a more unified approach.

Jonathan believed brands such as Thrust would come out of the petrol price war strengthened and able to seize opportunities arising from the demise of weaker rivals. And although he was eager to expand Thrust's operations, he knew that Bayford could also benefit from the redevelopment potential of any surplus sites.

These two strategies influenced the way ahead for Bayford's fuel retail business. Firstly, Jonathan promoted the concept of franchising to expand the brand more rapidly across the country. It took him two years to persuade his father to let him implement the idea. Finally launched in 1998, franchising was offered to other independent regional oil distributors so they could in turn offer their customers the Thrust package. As Jonathan said at the time, 'If you want independence, what's your choice today? Most of the independent fuel supplies are now owned by oil companies ... we're saying to other regionally strong distribution companies, here's the Thrust brand, you have it, you sell it and we'll support it.' Jonathan asked his brother Paul, who had joined the business in 1995, to spearhead the concept as dealer

development manager. He signed up a number of regional distributors, including BWOC, Barton Petroleum, Chapter Oils, Eveson Fuels, GB Fuels, Nigel Collison Fuels, Southern Counties Fuels and, in Northern Ireland, Morgan Fuels. The scheme received a major boost in 1999 when Conoco Jet took a Thrust franchise for its authorised distributor network as a way of servicing its smaller rural sites more effectively.

Secondly, Jonathan began to push the idea of acquiring a much bigger rival operator as a way for Bayford to accelerate the expansion of its filling station operations and profit from realising the redevelopment value of any unwanted sites. Jonathan was certainly ambitious: the target he had in mind was Save Group. As one press profile of him observed at the time,

'The young gun of the family ... has already helped change the company's culture ... Thriving on ideas, ambition, enthusiasm and fun, Turner believes he can achieve all he wants at Bayford.'

Franchising manager Paul Turner (on the right) congratulating John Lovesay of Barton Petroleum on joining the Thrust franchise programme.

Investors in People

As a way of involving everyone in changing the way they worked, Jonathan and Liz were keen to use the Investors in People (IIP) quality assurance accreditation. IIP gave them the more formal mechanism they felt they needed to achieve change and win greater credibility in the business. The process got underway in 1997, led by Lorraine Lowe. A qualified trainer, with extensive personnel experience, she had been with the business since 1982.

The process illustrated just how important people were to the business. Outside facilitators encouraged team work, business planning and better systems. Employees welcomed proposals for improved training and development as well as better communications: an annual company meeting was successfully introduced, the first one held in August 1998, with six presentations over six days to every member of staff.

As part of the strategy of bringing people more closely together, Jonathan set up a unified sales team. All retail sales calls were channelled through a single sales department, and the sales team was relocated in a refurbished sales office equipped with much-needed new technology. A joint training course brought together the teams from sales and credit control and re-emphasised the message promoted by Jonathan and Liz Slater that the business should be a sales-led organisation. A revised management development programme underscored the ethos of a united business where everyone worked in the interests of the company as a whole, where every business unit was part of one organisation, all pulling in the same direction, each team working as one alongside each other.

Slowly, the culture changed, as the company became driven by sales and marketing. Change extended across the business, from drivers, who became part of the front-line sales team, equipped with uniforms and name badges, with responsibility for their own customers, to the credit control and accounts teams, who were encouraged to move from being 'sales-prevention officers' to a more positive sales-led approach. 'We needed people on our bus,' said Jonathan, 'who got the dream and the vision ... Those that didn't get on the bus went. It was just a generational thing – the people were lovely – but Liz and I felt that if they couldn't operate at our pace, they were on the wrong bus.'

In 1999, the business achieved IIP status, retaining it ever since. The Gator received the plaque on 18 June. It was, said Lorraine Lowe, a great achievement given the diversity of the group's businesses and she pointed out that 'the company now has some good business practices in place that the directors and management team can continue to build on'. The company's IIP assessor noted that everyone she had spoken to enjoyed working for the company and that it was now a place where things were constantly improving, with management listening more, and people properly involved in developing the business. At last, barriers between different levels and between departments were coming down.

The Gator receives the Investors in People award for Bayford in 1999, surrounded by senior team members, including David Turner, John Turner, Andrew Turner and - as the Gator - Jonathan Turner.

1999-
2004

Save Group had been badly hit by rampant price cutting in the industry. The business was making little money and the share price was falling. Yet it was still the UK's largest chain of independent filling stations.

The Save Group Deal

Jonathan began by finding out from James Frost whether or not he was willing to sell. When he said he was, Jonathan then had to work out how Bayford was going to pay for the business. There was a risk, but for Jonathan it was a calculated risk and he was certain that the returns from the deal would be significant. The idea was put to the Bayford board in 1999, the year in which Jonathan and Liz both became directors, Jonathan as commercial director, Liz as sales director. Jonathan's proposal that Bayford should have a major stake in a new company set up for the purpose of the

acquisition won support from several of his colleagues, but his father proved difficult to persuade.

Negotiations dragged on for months. Jonathan's position was not helped by the 29.9 per cent stake taken by veteran property tycoon Jack Petchey, whose investment buoyed up Save Group's share price. On the one hand, this encouraged Bayford to sink funds into its own significant stake in Save Group; on the other, it sowed doubt in the minds of Jonathan's fellow board members about the viability of his scheme.

But Save Group was living on borrowed time – although it never made a trading loss, it was consistently under-investing in order to achieve a profit and fund dividends – and on 28 February 2001 it went into administration with debts of £95 million. Again, Jonathan saw this

as an opportunity – he proposed borrowing to buy the Group out of administration – but again his colleagues were lukewarm. The collapse of the Group seemed to confirm the view that the general outlook for the industry was very gloomy, yet here was Jonathan suggesting they invest in several hundred filling stations. Their decision did nothing to dampen his enthusiasm for the deal. 'When everyone's going in one direction, I'll go in the opposite direction; if someone tells me to turn left, I'll turn right; if someone says no, I'll say yes.'

'If someone tells me to turn left, I'll turn right; if someone says no, I'll say yes'

It was James Frost, eager to save as many of the Group's jobs as possible, who advised Jonathan to sound out Jack Petchey about putting together a bid. Jack Petchey's incentive would be to recoup the losses made on his substantial shareholding (Bayford too had lost all its money). A meeting was eventually arranged between the two men. In return for a 20 per cent share of the equity, Jonathan told Jack he would run the business on a day-to-day basis while the assets were gradually sold off. Jack quietly pointed out that Jonathan had no money to invest, and neither did Bayford, in which Jonathan didn't even own any shares. In other words, Jonathan was asking him to shoulder all the risk while giving away a fifth of the returns. 'So,' recalled Jonathan, 'I was really negotiating from a position of significant weakness and I didn't really know whether I could do what I said I would do since I'd never done it before.'

The deal was saved when Jonathan proposed that in any new company set up to take over Save Group, Bayford would transfer its own filling stations at their balance-sheet value of £3 million. He also reduced from 20 to 10 per cent his request for an equity stake in the deal. Jack Petchey agreed: he recognised the value of combining Jonathan's knowledge of fuel retailing and his own organisation's property expertise.

For Bayford, where the filling stations were losing money, it was a lifeline. Ultimately, Jonathan believes, it saved the business. In May 2001, the board willingly agreed to the proposal. His family, Jonathan recalled, couldn't believe it: Bayford was getting full balance-sheet value, effectively full value, for the poorly performing filling stations it was transferring to the new company. Bayford would earn 10 per cent interest on the company's investment and the capital would be repaid through loan notes. Jonathan estimated the company would receive £5 million after three years based on a £29 million profit from the disposal of Save Group's sites. In fact, the actual profit turned out to be nearly twice as much.

There would be one more hitch before the deal was done. Jonathan discovered another bidder was ahead of him in the queue. Anglo Petroleum, part of Bermuda-based Sutton Oil, owned by Paul Sutton, was poised to buy Save with a bid of £55 million, having paid a non-returnable deposit of £2 million. When the announcement was made, it was a blow for Jonathan: 'All the work, the effort, excitement, potential gain, all lost.' But Sutton's business dealings were rarely straightforward, and the financial backing he claimed to have for the deal proved illusory. Instead, the administrator accepted Jonathan's cash offer of £47 million plus £7 million for stock on condition contracts were exchanged in six weeks. All the cash came from Jack Petchey; Jonathan was stunned that the deal involved no debt whatsoever.

The public announcement of the deal was made on 25 November 2001 and completion was achieved on 10 January 2002. At eleven o'clock that night Jonathan found himself in Tony Sharp's office at KPMG, with Jack Petchey on one phone and the administrator on the other, as the final details were agreed. As he later remembered,

'And it happened and the phone went down and I just looked at Tony with tears in my eyes. I'd just negotiated to buy the biggest independent chain of petrol retailers in the UK with £47 million of somebody else's money.'

The new company formed to take over Save Group was called Save Retail Ltd. It absorbed Save Group's 409 sites and Bayford's 8. Jack Petchey's managing director, Ron Mills, drew up a disposal programme aimed at selling as many sites as quickly as possible to raise cash. By the autumn of 2002, only the last hundred and most difficult sites remained unsold. While this was going on, Jonathan was appointed as managing director of the UK's biggest filling station operator, working from a base in Aylesbury, helping to sell off sites in some of the more remote parts of the country. It was not an easy task: he had to contend with demoralised employees as well as fuel suppliers and hauliers whose business steadily diminished as more

Gerald Ronson

One of the disappointed bidders for the Save Group was another experienced property investor, Gerald Ronson, who was also well known for his chain of Heron filling stations. He was so curious to know more about this breezy young entrepreneur who had beaten him to a major deal in a sector in which he was a leading player that he rang him up. The phone call was completely unexpected as was the invitation Gerald extended to Jonathan to come down and meet him at his headquarters, Heron House, in Marylebone Road in London. Jonathan could not quite believe it. After all, Gerald Ronson was one of his business heroes, and here was Gerald interrogating him about his background and the deals he had done. Although they came into contact only sporadically after that first meeting, their paths would cross profitably some years later.

sites were sold off. By the time the last site was sold early in 2004, the majority were still operating as filling stations. The exercise raised £100 million, making a profit of £53 million for Jack Petchey, with Jonathan earning 10 per cent.

For Jonathan, said Liz Slater, looking back, the experience 'was almost like his rite of passage and it gave David and John a lot more confidence when he came back that he could run a business'. Jonathan was very aware of this. Still only in his thirties, he saw it as another

step in his relentless determination to move out of the shadows cast by his family and carve out his own identity as an entrepreneur and businessman. He was also aware just how important securing Bayford's participation in the Save Group deal was for the business. As his brother Paul told him, 'If it wasn't for you, we would have gone bust.'

The Gulf Deal

But the Save Group deal was not the only significant venture with which Jonathan was involved. Equally significant for Bayford's retail fuel business was the deal that came along at the end of 1999. Jonathan was always a fervent believer in the value of networking and he was already well known in the industry. One morning he took a call from Meg Annesley, the chair of the Association of United Kingdom Oil Independents. She had been approached by a group of businessmen who wished to reintroduce a leading fuel brand to the UK. They told her that they believed Jonathan was the person to help them do that and they wanted to set up a meeting.

The brand was Gulf, which had been one of the country's leading brands until it had been bought a couple of years earlier by Shell, who killed it off. For Jonathan, one of the great things about Gulf was its long and successful association with motorsport. He agreed to meet the businessmen concerned at their offices in London close to Buckingham Palace.

The meeting that took place in April 2000 would be the first of many as negotiations for a joint venture got underway. It was a great opportunity, Jonathan told his colleagues at the beginning of 2001, to link Bayford with one of the best-known brand names in the sector.

'If it wasn't for you, we would have gone bust'

The Gulf deal was a lifeline for Bayford's retail fuel business. For several years Jonathan had taken every opportunity to protest at the way the major oil companies were discriminating against independent operators through two-tier pricing even though he knew little could be done to prevent the oil companies and supermarkets from selling below the wholesale price paid by smaller distributors. As a result, Bayford had been closing Thrust filling stations as had its franchisees. Jonathan was convinced that the Gulf brand would help Bayford to compete in the fuel retail market in a way that Thrust had never been able to do. 'The Gulf brand,' he told them, 'is the only option for us in the retail market because we cannot sell the Thrust brand.'

Given the poor state of the sector, his colleagues, including his father, were understandably sceptical, and Jonathan had to argue long and hard to persuade them of the deal's merits. He never wavered in his own belief in the deal. As he told one industry journal, the market was

'a complete nightmare at the moment and if we are to remain in it, we need to be wearing the right colours. This is a tremendous opportunity for us to work with a global business with a passionate brand ... We can't just bury our head in the sand and hope the storm will blow over. We have to get out there and do something different. It's called innovate or die!'

By the end of 2001, a deal had been done. A licensing agreement covered fuel and lubricants and two new companies were formed, Gulf Lubricants UK Ltd and Gulf Retail UK Ltd, in which Bayford and Gulf Oil International, a subsidiary of the Hinduja Group, were partners. The operation was a wholly network-based operation, managed entirely by the new company. Bayford re-launched the brand at the Forecourt Show in April 2002 with the ambitious aim of having 200 branded sites by the end of the year.

'The Gulf brand is the only option for us in the retail market'

Meeting the Hinduja Brothers

Jonathan knew he was meeting the Hinduja brothers to discuss the Gulf brand but he knew little about them: there was no internet; he was very busy with the Save deal; and he simply had no time to do any research. Founded in India in 1914, the Hinduja Group was one of the world's largest conglomerates, employing 70,000 people worldwide. The Hinduja brothers themselves, Srichand and Gopichand, were reputedly the wealthiest people in the UK. It was Gopichand's son Sanjay who met Jonathan that spring morning. Jonathan hardly let Sanjay get a word in edgeways as he proceeded to tell him what a great opportunity it was, wagging his finger at him, telling him what could be done and what they could do together. The meeting, he thought, had gone well.

And then in the lift going down, the brothers' lawyer, Farooz Shahami, turned to Jonathan, and said, 'You don't know who these people are, do you?' He suggested Jonathan might like to look them up in The Sunday Times Rich List. Third on the list were the Hinduja brothers: Jonathan could feel the goose-pimples standing up on the back of his neck. 'Oh, my God, I was sat in their office, telling them how to run their business, what an idiot!' In fact, Sanjay enjoyed the fact that Jonathan didn't really know who they were and wasn't intimidated by them.

The Yorkshire Oil Company

There were many opportunities to strengthen the oil distribution business, which was becoming the most profitable part of Bayford. When Liz Slater joined the board as sales director in 1999, she set out her continuing ambitions for the oil business. 'Our mission,' she later reflected, 'became to make oil the star ... we got a super-team together, and set our stall out, and said this business can make a million pounds.' Her pronouncement was met with disbelief, but she was right and the target was met within a year. She led a great team: 'They were a fantastic team of people who egged each other on and believed they could do anything. We had a fantastically willing team who would do anything and go anywhere for the cause.' Following Liz's appointment to the board, Mark Kilvington took over as sales manager with Chris Ritchie as assistant sales manager. To take over Mark's

marketing role, Rob Staines was recruited in 2000.

Jonathan was eager that Bayford should 'be continually on the lookout for new opportunities in areas where we have core skills. By the very nature of the diversity and independence of our operations, we can fill niches left by the oil companies and react to opportunities quicker.' In the summer of 2000, Bayford bought BP's regional petroleum business, Dominion Fuels, formerly Wayahead Fuels. The £245,000 purchase price was financed by the sale of property. It came with 20 employees and depots in Halifax, Sheffield and York. The latter depot once more took Bayford into East Yorkshire where it had not had a presence since an ill-fated joint venture in the 1980s. With seven depots around the county, Bayford was able to describe itself as the Yorkshire oil company.

With all these time-consuming projects, it is scarcely surprising that Jonathan found it difficult to concentrate on the day-to-day business, underlining how much he relied upon the team back at Bowcliffe Hall and elsewhere under Liz Slater. Their relationship was becoming fundamental to the business. While Jonathan was achieving recognition as Bayford's driving force, marked by his appointment as managing director in the summer of 2000, it was Liz with her command of detail who kept the company going day by day.

Together they were pushing to set more challenging boundaries for the business. Jonathan wanted more managers to question the status quo and widen their horizons by developing contacts with external organisations. Liz wanted directors and managers to become more accountable, measuring their performance against agreed objectives, accompanied by an improved career development programme to ensure the company retained talented individuals. She was critical of the time spent by the board fire-fighting under-performing parts of the business at the expense of those with

The Campaign for Leaded Petrol

A flyer promoting leaded petrol for classic cars, with a classic Jaguar being filled up by Rob Staines at the Bayford Thrust service station in Harewood, near Leeds.

Leaded Petrol

- High margin, niche product
- Gain a competitive edge over other forecourts in your area
- Support Britain's motoring heritage
- Listing for your site on www.leadedpetrol.co.uk
- Turn the phasing out of LRP to your advantage
- Take leaded petrol, no matter who supplies your main grades

www.leadedpetrol.co.uk

Despite all the major deals he was involved with, Jonathan still found the time and energy to lead a successful campaign to make sure that leaded petrol remained available to owners of vintage and veteran vehicles. In 1999, the UK government announced that leaded four-star petrol would no longer be sold on forecourts from 1 January 2000. There were very good reasons for the ban related to the impact of lead in the air on health. Jonathan joined with Lord Montagu of Beaulieu, Chairman of the National Motor Museum, which he had founded, and President of the Federation of British Historic Vehicle Clubs, who was able to raise the issue in the House of Lords. As a result, the government agreed to allow limited supplies of leaded petrol to remain available. It was difficult to obtain suppliers, difficult to retain them and, ultimately, sales didn't meet expectations, but Bayford continued to supply leaded fuel for enthusiasts until 2008. It did, however, do wonders in terms of publicity for the business. 'It was another way of putting Bayford on the map,' said Jonathan, 'and we became the only company supplying leaded petrol in the UK.'

Bayford and the Fuel Blockade

The oil business faced a major challenge during protests against the rising price of fuel in the autumn of 2000. On Monday, 11 September, remembered Mark Kilvington, the company began sending people out to the depots and filling stations, trying to keep things calm and controlled. The company's newsletter reported that 'the fuel crisis brought out the best in everyone and it was fantastic to see everyone pulling together'. Retail employees were brilliant in handling customers who clogged the forecourts solidly for three consecutive days, while sales teams at the Hall and the depots handled a seemingly never-ending stream of telephone enquiries. Drivers 'performed miracles with the volume of deliveries they achieved since the blockades were lifted'. For instance, a tanker appeared at the Burley Road filling station within 45 minutes of the station running out of unleaded fuel on a Saturday afternoon with two-hour-long queues. The biggest challenge was persuading tanker drivers to carry on because of the intimidation they faced: at one depot, the driver turned up with his friend, both wielding baseball bats for self-protection. 'It was pretty scary, to be honest,' admitted Mark Kilvington. Other members of staff also faced intimidation and at least one was assaulted. Attempts at queue-jumping at the filling stations were common but on the whole the queues were peaceful, speaking volumes for the way team members handled things.

Liz Slater recalled how protestors also blockaded the depots. 'We did such a good job charming our protestors that we continued to operate.' Team members helped to direct traffic, and then late at night Liz invited all the protestors to join them for fish and chips. She later received a letter from them thanking her for the way they had been treated. Treating people well paid off for she was able to persuade them to allow tankers to deliver fuel for the most critical cases. 'A great time and a great team.'

Widespread protests at the price of fuel took place during the summer of 2000.

(Adrian Sherratt/Alamy)

profitable potential. She reviewed crucial areas of the business, including health and safety, where accountability was essential. Jonathan, Liz, and Chris Dean, the group accountant and company secretary, all believed the management team needed strengthening, and Jonathan was pressing for the appointment of an operations manager to free up time for himself, Liz and Chris.

The drive to promote a more positive culture in the business was relentless. In 2002, when the business was rebranded as Bayford, moving away from the Thrust name in the light of the Gulf deal, it was accompanied by a formal set of core values, displayed throughout the company. People were at the heart of these values, whether employees, customers or the wider community, as was the building of relationships, from fulfilling customer expectations to effective team working. As Jonathan was reported as saying at the time,

'the key differential has to be the people at Bayford ... What differentiates us all is the way in which we treat and approach the customer. We are striving to have a strong management team that can lead from the front. We must show all our employees that to survive profitably in the market place we have to think quicker and smarter than the rest.'

It was an ethos shared by Liz Slater. 'The people I work with are like a family to me,' she would say a few years later. 'They are very caring and they are extraordinarily dedicated to the business. At Bayford we make the effort to get to know our colleagues, and people here feel they are part of something special.'

Bayford's core values highlighted the importance of passion and commitment in achieving success and emphasised professionalism, respect and accountability. They also encapsulated the approach Jonathan and Liz had embraced since they had joined Bayford. As Jonathan had said in the company newsletter on his appointment as managing director, 'We will continue to build a business that will provide enjoyment and long-term security for all within it. I want everyone to enjoy what they do – life is too short and we spend plenty of time at work!' As Liz recalled,

'I always knew what I wanted to do with the business. I could close my eyes and see it. There was nothing more scientific about it. We had brilliant people and we could do anything we wanted to do. And if you do it once, and it works, you get a bit more ambitious, and that works too! We would always start with the end; none of the detail started until we knew what the result looked like.'

Fambo

Jonathan's achievements since the late 1990s, combined with his commitment to the business, left his father, David, and his uncle John convinced that he was the right person from the next generation to lead the business. It was a view shared by other observers too. As Bob McNaughton, Bayford's audit partner, noted,

'Jonathan was the shrewdest of them all and could drive a good bargain. He was charming and easy to get on with. I could see he would take the business to the next stage and it needed that.'

Since his appointment as managing director, Jonathan had been pushing for a deal that gave him freedom. In everything he did, Jonathan wanted to be his own person. Just as he had been determined to carve out his own identity to free himself from being known as his father's son, so he had no wish to inherit the business. To be given the company would run completely counter to everything he had ever striven for. What he wanted to do was to buy Bayford.

'It was all about self-esteem – I did not want to inherit anything, I did not ... I'd done a few deals, I was starting to get some credibility with the business community and with the oil companies and suppliers and the banks, and people were starting to wake up and think "Oh, this guy's rocking and rolling, I might lend him some money." I didn't want anyone to think I'd been given anything, that I'd had a leg up, that I'd inherited anything.'

For that reason, Jonathan wanted any deal to be at arm's length. He proposed buying the business for its net asset value of £7 million at a time when it was making around £200,000 net profit. For an indebted business in an uncertain industry, it was more than a fair offer. It was, suggested Tony Sharp, who was again advising Jonathan, substantially more than was justified on a multiple of earnings basis, but it was an indication of Jonathan's self-belief that he could do great things with the business. The quid pro quo was that the purchase price was deferred, settled by the redemption of loan notes over several years.

In principle, David and John Turner were not opposed to the idea, which became known as Fambo, shortened from Family Buy Out. After all, the brothers had done exactly the same thing nearly 30 years earlier. And they were anxious to prevent Jonathan's departure, although Jonathan himself had discounted that option. They also knew that the timing was right; by 2000, David was in his early sixties, John in his early fifties. Extensive consultations were undertaken with other family members and numerous options were discussed, including a sale to outside investors or doing nothing at all. Ultimately, it was agreed that the best interests of everyone concerned lay in selling the business to Jonathan.

Family considerations determined that the deal took four years to complete. Jonathan's greatest supporter throughout the negotiations was his uncle John, who was certain in his own mind that Jonathan had to be given the chance to own the business. As Tony Sharp recollected,

'Through all of this John was totally supportive; without John, this deal could never have happened. John's commitment to it was quite amazing.'

Finally, in February 2004, Jonathan Turner became the sole owner of Bayford & Co Ltd through a new company called Fambo Ltd. Jonathan's comments to a journalist in 2006 reflect the mixed feelings any son and nephew might have in taking over from his father and uncle a business that existed largely because of their efforts over the course of a previous generation:

'They felt I was the right person to lead the business. They believed in me and I think I have repaid that trust by driving the business forward and continuing their success. My game plan was always to take charge of my own destiny. My self-esteem has always been important for me and I wanted to be recognised on my merits.'

David Turner remained chairman until his death in 2008, and John Turner also stayed on the board. As Jonathan told one magazine,

'The strategy we followed means that the business is still within the family: we still work together; the family can still be passionate about it; they still have an input, but they don't have the risk. The credit for all that rests with my father and uncle for the way they handled such a delicate issue.'

2004-08 8

Jonathan was 'massively enthusiastic and bouncing around, full of incredible ideas'

Once Jonathan became the sole owner of Bayford & Co Ltd, he and Liz Slater were eager to press on with the approach they had been following for the past few years. 'We both knew what we wanted,' said Liz, 'and although we might each have gone about things differently, it didn't change the end result.' They wanted to stabilise the business, expand it, improve its performance and make it more profitable; the key to this, they both believed, was enthusing people, motivating them, paying them well and rewarding them in unusual ways.

The Bayford Team

The team they built up was crucial to Bayford's success over the next few years. Jonathan invited Tony Sharp to act in an informal role as advisor to the board.

Regularly attending Monday morning management meetings, Tony observed how their friendly, relaxed and informal nature encouraged people to speak their minds. Having appointed his team, Jonathan, reflected Tony Sharp,

'knew they were different from him; he knew they would make life difficult for him, but he put them in place. He was prepared to accept he might get a rough ride from them from time to time but he knew they were essential to running the business day-to-day, which he had moved away from.'

Jonathan never shied away from criticism, and his team reined in some of what they regarded as his wilder ideas, just as his father had been restrained from time to time by his uncle.

In 2003, Jonathan had appointed James Spencer as operations director. After several years' experience with BP, James was eager to return to the world of operational management. Bayford, said James, 'had just bought the Gulf brand and it was going places'. He found Jonathan Turner to be 'massively enthusiastic and bouncing around, full of incredible ideas, and I came away impressed with this enthusiasm, which I was missing at BP. He was a hugely enthusiastic guy; he had a great sense of humour; he's always been a slightly irreverent person, and I liked that.' Liz, on the other hand, 'was very focused, very precise, knew what needed to be done, knew her managers needed structure around them to make them easier to manage'. Jonathan and Liz complemented each other and got on well.

In 2005, Phil Hall joined the team as finance director. His appointment was seen as a major coup for Bayford since Phil had been managing director of CPL, a major rival; for Jonathan, it was another seismic moment. Phil was able, knowledgeable and credible, in turn lending greater credibility to the business. 'Phil and I could go anywhere,' said Jonathan, 'and talk to anybody about buying a business with great credibility; with my ability to tell a story and his ability to back me up, we were a really, really great team.' Phil, too, admitted Jonathan, never hesitated to keep him in check. 'I used to ring Phil, and he would lift the receiver and just say, 'No', and put the phone down.'

This quartet, Jonathan, Liz, James and Phil, shared the same office for some time and, said Jonathan,

'There is no doubt about it, that between 2004 and 2009 we were the dream team and whatever we did, wherever we went, whatever we touched, it just worked.'

An Unnerving Encounter

James Spencer had one unnerving moment soon after he joined Bayford. He turned up at Bowcliffe Hall very early one morning, around quarter past five, ready for an early start, but found he couldn't get into the building. It was a misty October morning with no one around, or so he thought, as he heard the gravel crunching behind him. Out of the fog emerged big Dave Ormerod with his shotgun. By then Dave had been with the company for nearly 30 years, originally as a tipper driver, hauling coal from the pits to the power stations, before moving to general maintenance. James had never met him and had no idea Dave had been out shooting rabbits at David Turner's request. 'I was just seeing some big guy, looking like a weird Yorkshire gillie, with hat and a knackered Barbour jacket and cheap wellies, with a rifle, walking towards me, and I absolutely thought, "Well, that's it then." And he said, "Who are you then?", and I said, "I'm James Spencer, the new operations director." "Never heard of yer." Anyway, he put his rifle down, didn't shoot me and eventually let me into the building, and I got on with some spreadsheets.'

As he told *The Yorkshire Post* in April 2006,

'The business has got a whole lot better since I stopped dabbling in the detail. I now work on the business rather than in it and am lucky that I have such a great team alongside me that allows me to do that.'

Jonathan was admitting that he was no longer fulfilling the role of managing director. The person filling that role was Liz Slater. In 2007, Jonathan took the title of chief executive and Liz became managing director. 'We got to a stage,' said Jonathan,

'when we realised that Liz would be a much better MD than me. We learned that Liz was much better at running businesses than me, much better at managing people, much better at the details, much better at getting things done. I'm the entrepreneurial, creative, hand-grenade thrower, creating carnage everywhere, and she's the dustpan and brush, who sweeps it all up and puts order into it.'

Liz recalled how Jonathan, when he was managing director, came to realise that

'it wasn't a job he wanted to do: he's far too unstructured, off on to the next thing, and blah, blah, blah. And we had quite a big business then, and it needed a bit of structure, a bit of discipline, things I could bring to the party.'

Jonathan and Liz encouraged a team ethos from the top to the bottom of the business. As Jonathan told *Fuel Oil News* in January 2006, 'We put a lot of effort into making sure our employees enjoy themselves.' He was referring to the Las Vegas-themed fancy-dress party held on New Year's Eve at Bowcliffe Hall, where a marquee had been turned into Caesar's Palace, complete with palm trees, statues and gaming tables. Jonathan, Liz, James and Phil were dressed in purple leotards, fishnet tights, feather boas and head plumes.

John Turner and Chris Dean on the left and Jonathan Turner on the right all dressed up to enjoy one of Bayford's fancy dress parties.

In 2006 and 2007, Bayford featured on *The Sunday Times* list of the 100 Best Small Companies to Work For. 'Having fun at the same time as meeting corporate objectives is the bottom line for the company,' said the paper. Jonathan Turner was seen as an inspiring leader by more than 80 per cent of his employees. The same proportion said they had fun working with their team, were confident in their colleagues and believed the company was a caring place to work. In the words of *The Yorkshire Post*, 'The Bayford culture is one of fun and enjoyment while exceeding clear goals and objectives.'

Spot bonuses and away days rewarded outstanding individual and team contributions.

Success in meeting annual company targets gained every employee an extra holiday on their birthday. A 'Live the Dream' scheme helped employees achieve goals outside their work. Newcomers were given the chance to dine informally with the directors and were allotted a mentor for their first six months. There were opportunities for flexible working and job swaps.

'The Bayford culture is one of fun and enjoyment while exceeding clear goals and objectives'

Celebrating inclusion in the Sunday Times 100 Best Small Companies To Work For list in 2007: left to right, Jonathan Turner, Andrew Turner, Tony Sharp, Phil Hall, Lorraine Lowe, Chris Ritchie, Alan Downing, Adam Walsh, Liz Slater and James Spencer.

Liz Slater was central to all this. As Rob Staines recalled, 'She gave you time; she showed her concern; she remembered your birthday; she sent you cards to pick you up when you were down.' The 'dream books', in which people pasted images depicting their own aspirations, were also her idea. When Rob had the chance to accompany his father to Australia for the Rugby Union World Cup in 2003 with tickets for the semi-final and final, he wasn't sure if the business could spare him for three weeks in November, one of the busiest times of year. Liz was unhesitating in telling him he should go and fulfil one of his ambitions.

Jonathan Turner was clear about the value of the ethos he summed up as 'having fun and making money'.

'We believe that people rarely succeed at anything unless they have fun doing it. We don't do boring. We have a unique culture where personality counts as highly as ability and we make sure that our people have a good time. This feeds through to our customers, suppliers and all our stakeholders. We aim to fill our businesses with people we trust to do the job and we let them get on and do it without interference. We thrive in an atmosphere where everything is an opportunity and we encourage people to challenge the mundane and predictable. We are very focused though innovative at the same time. If you don't know where you are going, how can you expect to get there?'

The years immediately after Fambo were exciting. Borrowing was easy and the economy was buoyant. Annual economic growth was averaging nearly 3 per cent, unemployment had fallen as low as 2.3 per cent in 2001, and inflation dipped to 2.2 per cent by the end of 2005. Despite the blip caused by the collapse of the dot-com boom in 2000, this was a period of remarkable economic stability. Acquisitions multiplied – in one year there were nine – funded by bank borrowings, earning Bayford the title of 'Acquirer of the Year' in 2006. One was the Petroplus fuel card business, which raised Bayford's profile in the industry. 'We were trying to set the world on fire,' said Chris Ritchie. Jonathan's ambition was obvious.

At that time the banks were great. I was able to borrow money from the banks to do lots of deals. I was doing things my father and my uncle didn't want to do: I was taking risks; I was borrowing money; I was buying businesses.'

> ## 'We were trying to set the world on fire'

But risks were always carefully calculated and Jonathan knew he could rely on his supporting team to handle the details of any acquisition.

Oil

Bayford was structured around four business units: oil distribution, fuel cards, petrol retailing, and property. The oil division continued to prosper, benefiting from James Spencer's expertise as operations director. Responsible for buying, transporting and pricing fuel, he created a mini-supply trading desk, an internal supply division, based on his BP experience. He introduced the idea of a transfer price, which gave the sales team consistent pricing and

created two profit streams: one from the profits made by sales on a daily basis, based on the transfer price set by the supply desk; and one based on the margin between the price at which supply bought the fuel and the internal transfer price. 'The sales team were freed up just to sell, and that model was absolutely, in my opinion, the core behind a very successful six years' trading.' James also changed the division's purchasing policy, switching to contract buying, which gave the reliability that ensured the seamless operation of managing stocks, from shipping in the fuel to the depots to shipping it out to the customers.

Most of Bayford's acquisitions were split between oil distribution and fuel cards. Additions to the oil business included Delta Fuels in Kendal, John Ellis Fuels in Wales, and Askham Fuels in Penrith. By 2006, the oil business was making deliveries from 8 depots to more than 30,000 businesses, farms and homes in northern England and northern Wales. Some of the depot managers, such as Rob Staines and Sue Florence, were outstanding.

Rob had originally joined to take over the marketing of the division from Mark Kilvington in 2000. Liz Slater spotted potential in this

A Day in the Life of a Tanker Driver

For many years Bayford's reputation for customer service depended upon the tanker drivers who delivered fuel to customers large and small the year round. As Motor Transport related in 1980, 'The choice of driver is considered of paramount importance. He must be a good ambassador for the company, with a detailed knowledge of the particular area, especially in the remoter areas of the Dales; completely trustworthy – any of the smaller deliveries are made without the customer being in attendance – and he must have an extremely comprehensive knowledge of the products he carries ... To attract the right sort of driver, every attempt is made to provide first-class vehicles, working conditions and a reasonable standard of reward. Labour turnover among drivers is extremely low, probably about 5 per cent, and has remained so for some time.'

Tanker drivers were highly skilled. Responsible for driving 20,000 litres of highly explosive fuel around the countryside, they paid careful attention to health and safety. They were adept at manoeuvring their vehicles into spaces most people would be reluctant to take a small car. Delivering petrol was a complex operation: as one journalist accompanying one of Bayford's drivers described in 2007, it 'calls for both a fuel delivery hose and a vapour recovery hose to capture the vapour driven out of the tanks by the incoming fuel. If you don't collect the vapour, it could burst the tank or even explode.' They had to cope with all types of destinations for deliveries, from police stations and council sites to businesses and private homes. Many drivers were long-serving, spending 20 years or more with Bayford, and they loved their job. Best of all, according to one of them, was 'the relationship ... built up with customers'. And it was true, said the journalist who accompanied him, that 'he was on extraordinarily friendly terms with everyone we had delivered to'.

slightly truculent young man, and within a year he had been despatched to run the newly acquired Sheffield depot, which had been losing customers. (Looking back, Rob appreciated his weaknesses as a young manager, once asking Liz why she had kept him on. It was because, she told him, she could see through his faults just how much he cared about the business and how much he wanted it to succeed.) A tragic international event, the 9/11 disaster, boosted business as people panicked, searching everywhere for available fuel supplies. Business quickly doubled and most of those customers stayed with Bayford. Four years later, Rob was running all the depots in tandem with Mark Kilvington

Fuel Cards

In 2003, Bayford launched Countrywide Fuel Cards, based in Wakefield, to sell BP fuel; and InterCity Fuel Cards, based in York, to sell Shell fuel. Half a dozen existing businesses were added over the next few years, including Truckhaven, Central, and Routemate. This epitomised, said the local newspaper, 'Bayford's aggressive programme of growth'. As one manager commented, 'If you just dabble in selling fuel cards, you won't do well. The essentials are a business plan, the right IT, telesales staff and account managers to look after the customers. It's about looking for business but also adding value in the marketplace.'

In 2006, all the fuel card businesses were folded into a separate subsidiary, The Fuelcard Company UK plc, based in Wetherby. It was the fastest-growing fuel card business in the

Team Rewards

Every target met by the oil distribution team was rewarded. After achieving their first profits target, they were told to stand by at their homes first thing on the Monday morning. Each of them was given a particular dress code: Mark Kilvington turned up in sunglasses and shorts, Rob Staines in a tuxedo. A stretch limousine collected them and soon they were heading for Blackpool. Stopping at Birch Services, Mark made out he was the security guard for recent lottery winner Rob, hence the tuxedo and limousine, as he pointed out to a group of increasingly excited older ladies on a coach trip. Achieving their second target earned the team four days at Euro Disney in specially printed black T-shirts bearing the slogan, 'Millionaires' Club'. 'Those were just amazing times,' said Rob, 'the camaraderie, the togetherness, it was great working as a team.' On another occasion the team were asked to come as their pop star of choice – Rob Staines, for instance, masqueraded as Boy George, Mark Kilvington as Adam Ant – 'and off we went,' recalled Liz Slater, 'champagne in hand, to this recording studio, and recorded songs all day long, and cut a CD, which was the worst CD ever'.

country. Managing 300 million litres of fuel, it was the only one to have partnerships with the UK's three biggest fuel brands: BP, Esso and Shell.

Such rapid success attracted outside attention. Jonathan became aware that private equity houses were investing in fuel card businesses. One of them, Bain Capital, which already owned a major global fuel card business called Fleetcor, approached Jonathan to express an interest in

buying The Fuelcard Company. Bain flew Jonathan out to Boston for a meeting at its headquarters. He spent the night in the Four Seasons Hotel before travelling to Bain's office high up in one of the city's skyscrapers, where he was shown into the most enormous room to find a group of men earnestly discussing deals valued at billions. Jonathan was offered a much higher offer than he could have obtained from a UK suitor, which he accepted, recognising that the industry was undergoing a period of consolidation in the UK. The business was sold to Fleetcor in 2007. This underlined Jonathan's rational approach and lack of sentimentality where business decisions were involved.

The deal almost stalled when BP objected, regarding Fleetcor as a major competitor. The problem was solved by removing the fuel card businesses selling BP fuel from the deal, much to Jonathan's irritation at the time. It was, as it turned out, fortuitous. The remaining BP fuel card businesses were turned into another separate business called Be Fuelcards.

Gulf Retail

The Gulf-branded retail fuel operation was a profitable high-profile business but it struggled to meet ambitious targets. By 2009, there were 170 branded filling stations, compared with the target of 200 set several years earlier. Nevertheless, the average volume of fuel per active outlet was increasing, and support given to small independent rural operators was popular. Numerous failing forecourts gained a new lease of life thanks to the advice and support received from Gulf Retail.

A typical example was a small family-run outlet near Clacton in Essex in 2007, which was under threat from a recently opened Tesco filling station nearby. With slumping sales of fuel and merchandise, the owners asked for the advice of Gulf Retail's area manager, Steve White, who passed them on to Gulf's merchandising partner. The range of goods was expanded; an alcohol licence was obtained; an attractive new layout was installed; and over several months turnover multiplied.

In 2008, Gulf Retail won the Oil Company Initiative of the Year award for its in-store shop consultancy programme. In the same year, the brand returned to motorsport sponsorship, supporting two Aston Martin works cars at Le Mans, marking the 40th anniversary of Gulf Oil's first Le Mans victory. The Goodwood Festival of Speed that year celebrated Gulf Oil's racing history, featuring several cars, including the Ford GT40, Porsche 917 and McLaren F1 supercar.

All this activity paid off in terms of results. Turnover rose steadily from just over £191 million in 2004, reaching more than £452 million in 2008, with Bayford's net profits peaking at £2.3 million in 2006. But there were clouds on the economic horizon. The signs were already there if anyone looked. Although real incomes increased by a fifth, house price inflation was soaring and final salary pension schemes were becoming a thing of the past. The seeds were being sown not only at home but also overseas for the dramatic collapse that affected the world economy from late 2008.

2008
Onwards

9

Jonathan Turner clearly recalls the day in 2008 when he first realised the downturn was coming. For US oil giant Conoco, Bayford was its biggest UK customer. Conoco's global head of credit management had come over from the USA to listen to a presentation by Jonathan and his team. The event went really well. Then, a few days later, Phil Hall rang Jonathan and asked him if he had a spare £8 million. Almost overnight Conoco had halved Bayford's credit limit.

With hindsight, said Jonathan, it was obvious that the Americans could see a massive global recession was imminent. At the time, however, he said, 'We had to react rapidly, go to all our customers, rein in payment terms, turn down lots of business because we couldn't afford to trade. And we needed to find that £8 million.'

Selling the Oil Business

Other suppliers were soon following Conoco's example. Combined with falling interest rates, this reduced the income the company was able to earn on funds received from customers prior to settling accounts with suppliers. The slump in oil prices also affected the business. Bayford had been earning income from charging other people to store their oil at the group's Leeds depot, but this was only of interest to outsiders as a hedge against higher oil prices. With oil prices falling, the incentive vanished. This economic jolt forced Jonathan, Liz and their team to re-evaluate the business. It had been very successful, expanding substantially by organic growth and acquisition. That, the team concluded, was the disadvantage. As Liz Slater recalled,

'The business had become very big. It had a lot of people; we didn't really know people's names, and the things which had made us very successful were long gone, and we had to become more corporate, which has never suited us at all.'

'We couldn't remember who anybody was,' said Jonathan. 'Liz and I got to the point of asking, "Is this fun?" I didn't like the fact that I didn't know everybody. Our fuel card business was getting huge and all the boys and girls would say hello and I didn't know who they were.' The strength of the business, he believed, was 'selling oil and doing deals, but we were getting bogged down in processes, paperwork and worrying ever more about customers with long-term debts'.

More significantly, perhaps, the business had also reached its limits. It was turning over more than £400 million a year, operating from 14 locations and delivering 468 million litres of oil through a 60-strong tanker fleet. 'We couldn't really grow anymore,' reflected James Spencer, 'based on the available credit we had.' Further expansion was limited without more capital, which realistically could come only from outside the business. Without serious structural change, James believed, growth over the next five years would be difficult.

Once again, rather than wait for an offer, Jonathan set out to find a bidder. He courted GB Oils, Bayford's biggest rival and part of DCC, the major Irish industrial holding company. When Jonathan deliberately established a competing business in part of the country previously dominated by GB Oils, the latter's managing director, Donal Murphy, approached Jonathan. GB Oils made an offer not just for the oil distribution business but also for the Gulf fuel retail and lubricants operation. The two sides agreed on a price of £22.5 million and the deal was completed at the end of September 2009. From start to finish, it took just five weeks.

What Next?

The impact of the sale on the business was huge. The group's turnover fell from more than £411 million in 2009 to £141 million in 2010. The number of employees fell to just 45. Among those who left was James Spencer, eager to set up his own business. Phil Hall followed soon afterwards. As Jonathan put it, 'We went from a massive business, hundreds of millions of pounds of turnover, lots of people, lots of responsibility, thousands of phone calls and emails, busy, busy, busy, to pretty much absolute silence; it was really weird. I remember looking at my phone and looking at my emails, thinking, "What happens now?"'

Bayford still had a profitable and successful fuel cards business, Be Fuelcards, which moved into offices in Bowcliffe Road in Leeds in 2010. But for Jonathan the attraction had palled. It was something he had already done, something he no longer found challenging.

'So, I came to work a bit later and left a bit earlier, and probably played golf, and did all those things that other people were doing. And then I went into what I describe as a black hole, not being overly excited, not being on my game and not being pushed or challenged or surrounded by lots of people to motivate and

'A Very Emotional and Sensitive Sale'

Jonathan was not sentimental about businesses. Nevertheless, after ringing Donal Murphy to accept his offer for the oil business, he sobbed for half an hour. He cared more about people and it was this that made the decision to sell more difficult. It was, he said, 'a very emotional and sensitive sale ... we agonised over the decision to sell – our hearts told us not to, but our heads knew that selling was probably the right way forward. It was hugely emotional and there were lots of tears.' Many of the people involved had grown up with the oil and fuel retail businesses that had been the heart of the group for many years. As Jonathan told one journalist at the time, 'I have put my life and soul into this business and I care greatly about the welfare of the 155 people who work for Bayford Oil.' But, ultimately, he would base any decision whether or not to sell on sound business reasons. Jonathan acknowledged the advice he received from Phil Hall. 'Phil put us on the right track to help clear our heads,' Jonathan said at the time. 'He knows the business inside out and the real impact of the continuing recession.'

The announcement of the sale stunned people in the business as well as those in the wider industry. 'To a lot of people,' said Chris Ritchie, 'this business was Bayford Oil.' Jonathan was disingenuous when he told one reporter that there had been no intention to sell and that the offer was completely unsolicited. Within the company, it was a well-kept secret, known to just a handful of people. Jonathan recalled just how difficult it was to make the announcement. 'I remember walking into the management meeting in the Bowcliffe Room; there must have been 23 people in the team, really bloody gorgeous people that I cared a lot about,

and we'd been up all night doing the deal, signing this and signing that. And I sat at the end of the big long table next to Liz, and they were all sat there expectantly, thinking, wow, what have we done now? And I knew what they were thinking ... they were just a bunch of expectant school children waiting for me to come up with the next thing because I'd come up with twenty things before and they'd all been great. And I sat there and I told them that I'd just sold the business, and I just burst into tears, and I just walked out, I couldn't speak. Their faces, the sense of shock; two women at the end of the room burst into tears as well; the emotion was beyond overwhelming. Liz came to get me and we had our little moment outside and then we went back in and held it together and explained why we'd sold the business. And that decision changed a lot of people's lives, unfortunately, and I knew that, but it was the right decision for the business. And with hindsight, with the impending financial crisis, it was definitely the right thing to do because we didn't really have any money; we were borrowing a lot of money; we were exposed to the oil companies with our credit limits, and the world was going mad.'

Following the sale, a touching response came from Mary Morrod, the wife of one of Bayford's tanker drivers. 'It must have been a very difficult decision for you to sell the company that you put your heart and soul into. I'm sure you did so with a great deal of sleepless nights and fretful days. [We] understand The Big Boys are always standing in the wings, and now whilst the company is in good shape has to be a very good decision on your part. We both wish you every good wish on your other bit of your company.'

excite. And that's what we used to do; we used to inspire people to do what they never knew they could do, but they weren't here anymore, and the phones weren't ringing, and I wasn't seeing my mates in BP and Shell or doing my wheeling and dealing. I felt I became a bit dull. I remember being at home thinking, "What am I going to do today?", feeling a bit lost, really.'

With money to invest, one idea was holiday rental properties. An offshoot, Decadent Retreats, was formed, comprising quality holiday-letting accommodation in the Northumberland coastal village of Bamburgh, where Jonathan and his wife, Karen, already had a holiday home. It was Karen who carried out the interior design and furnishing of each property. By then, they had three children: Freddie, born in 2000; Harry, born in 2001; and Olivia, born in 2003. The couple had met when they were teenagers and became friends when they were students in Newcastle. Jonathan proposed to Karen when she was his navigator on the Monte Carlo Rally in 1998.

In 2013, the company acquired the 13,000-acre Laudale estate in Scotland. Jonathan and Karen had been looking for a property in Scotland but the idea of taking over a substantial estate had never occurred to them. The estate agent, Savills, sent Jonathan details of the property. Its situation on the shores of Loch Sunart looked so stunning that Jonathan and Karen travelled up to visit the estate in December 2012. As well as a ten-bedroom house, the estate included a salmon farm, a mussel farm, deer stalking and six holiday cottages. The couple fell in love with the place and Jonathan agreed to buy it.

Karen and Jonathan Turner outside Bowcliffe Hall.

The next generation - Harry, Olivia and Freddie Turner in 2010.

Laudale.

The estate, which had been losing money, is now profitable; its operations have been reorganised; and the main house, furnished and decorated by Karen, is available for hire.

Guests are often flown in by seaplane. It is the most convenient form of transport for reaching Laudale, which can occasionally become inaccessible by road. Jonathan had never forgotten witnessing a magnificent seaplane in flight over Loch Lomond. He tracked down the owner, David West, and eventually they reached a deal: Jonathan would buy the plane and lease it back to David's business, Loch Lomond Seaplanes, which could continue to operate it commercially, with Jonathan hiring it when family or guests needed taking up to Laudale. In 2016, a new plane, a Cessna Caravan, was acquired and fitted with floats in Wichita, USA, with West flying it back to Scotland. It remains the only commercially available seaplane in Europe.

Something else the proceeds from the sale of the business allowed Jonathan to do was to completely refurbish Bowcliffe Hall and its grounds. With most of the remaining staff working out of offices in Leeds, there was potential to create high-quality office suites within the Hall itself. But Jonathan's vision went beyond commercial considerations. 'My vision,' he said, 'was to create unique offices with the look and feel of a country house home and put the character back in.'

The project was complex and had to meet multiple objectives: there had to be minimal interruption for existing tenants; a practical working environment, incorporating all the latest technology, had to be designed to attract

future tenants; and the scheme had to do justice to the architectural glories and historic value of the Hall and its setting. As one article summed it up, 'There was a strong vision to make Bowcliffe beautiful but it had to function as office suites with the amenities that would be expected in a modern building.'

The project became more complex as soon as it began, with the discovery of supporting beams where they were unnecessary and the lack of them where they were essential; walls that, unsurprisingly, were not straight; wiring and plumbing that hadn't been touched for years. The costs for the whole project were estimated to be £6.5 million. Joists and door frames were replaced, mouldings and door frames recreated. An interior design team visited similar properties seeking inspiration. Ultimately, 31 office suites were created inside the Hall.

In the grounds, impressive gates were added at the entrance to the Hall, and the expanse of car park immediately in front of the house, which had greeted visitors for years, was relocated to be closer to existing office buildings in the grounds. The whole area was returned to grass

'There was a strong vision to make Bowcliffe beautiful'

The Briefing Room and The Drivers' Club at Bowcliffe Hall.

with a gravel drive leading up to the house. Jonathan also renovated existing properties elsewhere on the estate, including Rosemount Cottage, which had almost fallen down, and the near-derelict but much loved and highly regarded cricket pavilion, converting them for future use as offices.

The most striking feature in the grounds is the million-pound Blackburn Wing, a tribute to the famous Yorkshireman who made Bowcliffe Hall his home for many years. Jonathan considered extending this aviation theme into the Hall by recreating a pilots' mess but instead harnessed his passion for vintage cars to create the Bowcliffe Drivers' Club. The magnificent head of a jaguar above one of the doors was spotted by Jonathan in the window of a London antique shop as he was taking a taxi to a business meeting. 'I have a mad passion for both old cars and interesting people,' Jonathan told the *Financial Times Magazine*, 'and the two often go together – so I decided to set up the Bowcliffe Drivers' Club as a place for enthusiasts to meet.' The club house reflects the British marques that make up most of Jonathan's own growing car collection. 'The requirements of membership are quite simple – you have to love old cars and be an interesting person. If you can manage that, you're in.'

The Blackburn Wing

As Jonathan developed his plans for Bowcliffe Hall, he became captivated by the story of aviation pioneer Robert Blackburn. In the summer of 2011, Jonathan had the pleasure of showing Robert's daughters Jane and Sarah around the Hall for the first time since they had left, following their father's death in 1955. From his interest in Robert Blackburn, and the emotional connection of the family with the property that was evident from his daughters, Jonathan conceived the fantastic vision of a giant tree-house in the Hall grounds, designed to look like an aircraft and big enough to host meetings and other functions.

In building this tribute to a famous Yorkshireman, Jonathan wanted to use Yorkshire architects, Yorkshire contractors and Yorkshire materials. He gave four Yorkshire architects the opportunity to tender for what he called 'a tree-house with an aviation theme'. It was a design based on a single wing from the Harris Partnership that caught his imagination.

Jonathan was advised by Mark Lane from DPP Planners in Leeds, and discussions were held with Planning Officer Adam Ward from Leeds City Council. Jonathan insisted on meeting Adam alone, which made his advisers anxious. But he wanted to enthuse Adam about his plans: 'This was emotional and he had to get it.' Jonathan himself was nervous since he knew that he depended upon Adam to turn his dreams into reality. Jonathan arranged to show Adam around the Hall and the grounds. When they came to the proposed site for the Wing, at the far side of the grounds, overlooking pastures and woodland, Jonathan began telling Adam about the Hall's links with Robert Blackburn. This immediately sparked Adam's interest since he had been involved with the application to build a supermarket on the site of the Blackburn factory, Olympia Works, in Leeds. This brought tears to Jonathan's eyes because he knew now there was a good chance his dream would become a reality. The path to planning consent was a long one, and numerous hurdles had to be overcome, but when the moment finally came, Jonathan was once again overcome with emotion.

Jonathan's chosen contractor was Neil Conlon, whose firm had an office in Harrogate. Jonathan was closely involved in the construction, and the foreman, Peter Carroll, could not have been more helpful. Jonathan, never really interested in details, realised he should have paid more attention to them when he stopped a wisteria-covered wall being bulldozed. The resulting copper and glass conference venue covering more than 2,000 square feet would cost the best part of a million pounds. The Blackburn Wing achieved a commendation from the regional branch of the Institution of Structural Engineers, which stated, 'This is a spectacular building, the structure of which impacts minimally on its ecologically sensitive surroundings.' In 2015, the Wing won RIBA's Yorkshire Award, and Jonathan the award for Yorkshire Client of the Year as well as a national award from the Royal Institute of Chartered Surveyors.

Robert Blackburn alighting from his Alvis car outside Bowcliffe Hall in the late 1940s.

Robert Blackburn beside the Type B monoplane before the start of the Aero Show Trophy Race at Hendon on 22 February 1913.

(© The Royal Aeronautical Society) (National Aerospace Library)/Mary Evans Picture Library)

BLACKBURN 33

BAYFORD
GROUP

Jonathan Turner, Frances Atkins, Roger Olive, John Tullett, Waldemar Guzik, Kirsty Beverley and Simon Crannage celebrating the acquisition of The Yorke Arms in Nidderdale in 2017.

(Tim Hardy Photography www.timhardy.co.uk)

The transformation of Bowcliffe was instrumental in clinching another property deal in 2017. When the Yorke Arms, the distinguished restaurant in Nidderdale, came up for sale, Jonathan was immediately interested: firstly, because of its reputation; secondly, because he and his team had enjoyed a memorable awayday and night there in the past. He met the owner and chef Frances Atkins and they quickly struck up a rapport. Although she wished to sell the property, she was eager to continue working. Jonathan invited her to visit Bowcliffe Hall and she was impressed with what she saw. They agreed Jonathan would buy and refurbish the property while Frances would stay on as the chef. Once again, Karen Turner breathed new life into the property, giving each of the 18 bedrooms a Yorkshire theme and commissioning as much work as possible from Yorkshire craftsmen and craftswomen. The restaurant reopened to rave reviews in the summer of 2018.

The Right Fuelcard Company

While Jonathan was taking more interest in property, Liz Slater was building up Bayford's remaining fuel card business, Be Fuelcards. As she remarked, 'Starting something from nothing and building it is what we do well.'

With this expansion, the Group appointed a new finance director. Tim Hall, a chartered accountant with extensive commercial experience, had been a friend of Jonathan's since they had been at prep school together. He was looking for a new opportunity just as Jonathan was looking for another finance director. As with Tim's predecessor, Phil Hall, Jonathan was looking for someone he could trust to manage the financial side of the business since, as he himself confessed, he never ever looked at a bank statement. Trust was absolutely essential and in Tim he had found the ideal candidate. A few years later, in 2017, Tim won the award for best finance director of a non-plc with turnover exceeding £50 million. The judges commented that 'he has delivered a vision and repeatedly analysed risks to make sure this happened'. He was an ideal partner for Jonathan.

In 2011, the opportunity came for the business to grow through acquisition. Gerald Ronson contacted Jonathan to invite him to join him in acquiring Total's UK business. As a result, through Gerald's investment vehicle, Rontec Investments, more than 800 retail sites were purchased from Total. But Jonathan and Liz knew that within the Total business lay another fuel card operation. This was moved out of the Total business and into The Right Fuelcard Company, incorporating Total's fuel card customers, as a joint venture between Jonathan, Liz and Gerald's Rontec business. Jonathan had succeeded in buying the business with which his father had done that deal nearly half a century earlier that had turned Bayford from a coal merchant into an oil distributor.

Having won Shell's agreement to launch a joint fuel card, increasing the business's accounts to more than 11,000, was a great opportunity for the business. Under Bayford's Adam Walsh as managing director, the previously loss-making operation was soon back in profit. Further fuel cards for Esso, Key Fuels and UK Fuels were subsequently added. By 2017, the business had 14,000 customers, turning over £137 million every year and making profits of more than £3 million. At the end of that year, Jonathan and

Liz sold their stake to Bayford, which remained a 50:50 joint venture since Rontec Investments retained its interest.

At the same time, The Right Fuelcard Company also acquired Be Fuelcards and another fuel card business, Diesel 24, set up in Scotland by Jonathan and his friends Campbell Brogan and Allan Tait. Combining all these activities within one company proved a shrewd move at a time when the UK fuel card industry was consolidating. With 27,000 corporate accounts and 150,000 card holders having access to 90 per cent of UK service stations, the business began to attract outside attention. An approach was made by a French company, Edenred, a specialist in prepaid corporate services. At the end of November 2018, Edenred agreed to buy 80 per cent of the business for £95 million, leaving Bayford and Rontec with 10 per cent each.

Gulf Gas & Power

For Jonathan, all this once again made business exciting. His enthusiasm had long since returned and he was eager to plot the future for Bayford. Debating the next move for the business, Jonathan, Liz and the rest of the senior team, Chris, Mark and Adam, concluded that oil was becoming yesterday's energy source. Here were shades of Fred Turner and his views about the coal industry 60 years earlier. They also believed that the use of fuel cards would fall as technology promoted the use of alternative payment methods. The answer, they felt, lay in the supply of gas and electricity and an approach was made to Shell.

An inspired suggestion came from Liz Slater. Bearing in mind how powerful the Gulf brand had been for Bayford in the past, why didn't Jonathan ask if Bayford could use the brand again for this new venture? 'That was like a mallet in Liz's hand,' said Jonathan, 'hitting me right in the face. I can't believe I didn't think about that first.' Meeting Jonathan for the first time in eight years, Sanjay Hinduja was only too happy to license the use of the brand. Jonathan even persuaded him to allow the new business to enjoy worldwide rights to the brand.

Initially, Jonathan was interested in acquiring an existing business in the UK and he had discussions with Luke Watson of GB Energy. Luke, the majority shareholder, disclosed to Jonathan that the business was actually in a lot of trouble. Within a few weeks, GB Energy had failed, making headlines in the financial press. Jonathan, however, reckoned that the lessons Luke learned from the fiasco would be invaluable and after Gulf Gas & Power UK was set up in 2018, Luke joined the company for a while.

Jonathan told Shell that he was also interested in setting up a similar business under the Gulf name in Europe. Shell introduced Jonathan and Liz to Michel Koornstra, Robin Van Klaveren and Edwin Hendrikse, who had considerable experience in the energy sector in the Netherlands. They came over to Bowcliffe Hall in 2016 and following months of negotiations agreed to invest with Jonathan and Liz in a new European venture. Gulf Gas & Power BV was set up in 's-Hertogenbosch in the Netherlands in 2018 with Shell as a business partner. Jonathan agreed to fund the €5 million Shell asked for as security from Bayford through a loan made possible thanks to the proceeds from the sale of his stake in the fuel card business.

The Business Today

Today, Jonathan Turner's business interests extend beyond Bayford, although the two merge together in people's minds. He remains an instinctive deal maker, who relies on his team to caution him against his wilder ideas and make done deals work. The force of his personality has helped the business forge alliances with major players in the industry, from Sanjay Hinduja and Gerald Ronson to BP, Esso and Shell. Combined with the growing professionalism of the business, fostered by Liz Slater and other senior managers, Bayford has earned the respect of the wider industry. 'And to have the respect of the industry,' reflected former Operations Director James Spencer, 'at the same time as being thought of as pretty good guys, that's quite a top achievement; in my experience, that doesn't happen very often.'

In May 2018, Jonathan appointed Lindsay Austin as Bayford's first externally recruited managing director. She came with extensive management experience in senior positions with Marks & Spencer, Mamas and Papas, Top Shop and Top Man. She was asked to take on the role effectively filled for many years by Liz Slater, helping to shape the business for the future and ensuring it operated efficiently day-to-day while making sure it retained the dynamism and agility to seize opportunities, which had served it so well in the past.

Lindsay now leads a team, including Tim Hall as finance director and Chris Ritchie as operations director, who make sure things happen once Jonathan has done a deal. 'Jonathan is great,' said Chris. While Bayford, he says, remains 'a small company playing in the big boys' league', Jonathan 'gets us to tables we should never be at, because he is absolutely blinkered when he gets an idea; nothing's too big, nothing's impossible'. While the business has had to become more corporate, it still has the characteristics of a family business. 'A lot of our success has been because we are a bit chaotic, a bit fleet of foot. We genuinely are a little bit different.'

Lindsay Austin with Liz Slater.

Tim Hall.

Bayford's achievements over the past 30 years are attributable largely to the outstanding business partnership between Jonathan Turner and Liz Slater. Although Liz is reducing her involvement, she remains committed to the business. For Jonathan, she has been indispensable.

'Liz is a huge part of the story. She's not family, but she is, because she's been here so long, and she's like my sister. I know that my father and my uncle respected her and valued her opinion. I am enormously in her debt, because I couldn't have done what I've done without her.'

'It's a brilliant relationship really,' says Liz.

'He refers to me sometimes as the sister he never had. He's very good at taking criticism and listening to all of my rants. I feel very entwined; I feel very vested in him and his success and in the business and its success. I feel very responsible for making sure that the business is as good as it can be. I shout at him a lot; some people would probably think we were 30 years married. There aren't many people you could work with for that length of time.'

For Tony Sharp, Jonathan's long-time advisor, Jonathan is

'an extreme entrepreneur, with tremendous energy for the business and for life. He is cavalier at times but he recognises that. And he completely turned around a tired business and changed it into a dynamic organisation. He is very good at building relationships within business. He's very loyal to his people.'

Jonathan Turner and Liz Slater with their teams at a tree planting ceremony in the grounds of Bowcliffe Hall in 2008.

He is, says James Spencer,

'an innately trusting person, which made him a great guy to work for, high on entrepreneurial testosterone, and at the end of the day that's what made him an interesting person'.

The human side of business has always been central to Jonathan's philosophy. It is perhaps the most fundamental aspect of the business and best characterised in the words of two long-serving members of the team, Julie O'Shaughnessy and Sally Genn. For Julie, 'Even when you've got tough times going on, when the people at the top are like they are, Bayford's have been there for us.' 'It's because of that,' added Sally, 'that you think, I'm going to work my socks off. And some of our closest friends have come through Bayford's. They manage to pick some really good people.'

Epilogue

After a century, the Bayford Group was at a crossroads. Where it went next was once more up to the enthusiastic and entrepreneurial chief executive who has shaped the business over the past 30 years. The Group's infant gas and electricity supply venture, giving Bayford its first toehold outside the UK, coupled with the proceeds from the recent sale of the fuel card business, gave Jonathan Turner plenty of scope for the future.

For some time, Jonathan had believed that the shift towards electrically-powered vehicles presented an exciting business opportunity, given the increasingly urgent need to construct an extensive network of vehicle charging points.

This led to Bayford, and Jonathan personally, investing in a public company called Fulcrum which was involved in utility infrastructure. Jonathan acquired his first Fulcrum shares in January 2019. Later in the year there was a possibility that in association with Macquarie, the major global investment bank, that Jonathan might accomplish a long-held ambition to acquire a public company and take it private. For a variety of reasons, this never materialised but Jonathan was approached by another significant investor, Harwood Capital, which in June 2020 led to Jonathan taking a seat on the Fulcrum board along with Harwood's Jeremy Brade as non-executive directors.

In the meantime, Jonathan was taking the Group's interests in the advanced energy sector in a different direction. In March 2020 Bayford partnered Smartest Energy UK to buy E Gas & Electric, a pre-pay supplier based in Birmingham with more than 300,000 energy accounts. The deal was something of a gamble, especially since only limited due diligence was possible, but Jonathan instinctively believed it was worth it. The negotiated price was just £250,000. The business came with 340,000 gas and electricity meter points, 165,000 customers and 170 employees. With all its customers on pre-paid terms, the business enjoyed an excellent cashflow. Historically it had been profitable and Jonathan believed that his team could turn it around, placing Chris Ritchie in day-to-day charge of running the operation.

Simultaneously, Jonathan's plans to create an electric vehicle (EV) charging business were reaching fruition. To help him, he approached

Jonathan Turner with his uncle John outside Bowcliffe Hall.

Paul Muncey, who had been instrumental in developing Gulf Retail and Gulf Aviation almost two decades earlier. Jonathan was able to negotiate an agreement for the use of the Gulf brand and the Gulf EV project was born. Taking its name from the Gulf logo, the business was called Orange Disc Ltd.

Then, all this activity was interrupted by the pandemic. A week after acquiring E Gas & Electric, most of its employees were asked to work from home as the first national lockdown was announced. As with so many other businesses, the lockdown also had adverse consequences for part of Bayford's own operations. The thriving hospitality business, centred on Bowcliffe and turning over £1.5 million, collapsed and the Bowcliffe Drivers' Club was forced to close. In the knowledge that the pandemic was likely to last some time, the sad decision was made to close the Yorke Arms

as a restaurant and convert it into a private country house for hire. With encouraging interest in lettings, this turned out to be a good decision.

Despite the turmoil caused by the pandemic, E Gas & Power is generating a lot of cash and returning to profit. With the business recently valued at around £15-20 million, Jonathan's calculated risk is paying off. The stake held by Jonathan and Bayford in Fulcrum plc continues to grow, having reached just over 14 per cent. In the belief that investing in an existing business would be a quicker route to success than starting from nothing in a fast-moving sector, Jonathan approached California-based ChargePoint, one of the world's largest makers of electric vehicle charging stations, which has led to discussions with one of ChargePoint's commercial partners in the UK about taking a stake in their operations.

In leading Bayford into new sectors of the economy, Jonathan epitomises the path taken by the business over more than a century. By adapting to changing circumstances, successive generations of the Turner family have steered a continuously evolving business through economic and other ups and downs, most recently characterised by the impact of the pandemic, let alone the uncertainty created by Brexit. Family businesses are fragile entities. To survive for a century or more as a successful organisation, like Bayford, is an outstanding achievement. For the future, perhaps, the key is to keep in mind those lessons from the past.

Timeline

Date	Events	People
1906		Fred Turner born
1919	Bayford & Co., coal merchants, founded around this time	
1922		Fred Turner joins Bayford
1923	Company based in Duncan St, Leeds	
1929	Premises taken at South Accommodation Road, Leeds	
1937	Bayford & Co. Ltd incorporated	
1938		David Turner born
1946		John Turner born
1958		David Turner joins the company
1964	Bayford signs oil distribution agreement with Total Oil Products	
1965	Bayford begins operating as an oil distributor	
1966		Jonathan Turner born
1967	Pepper Road leased	
1968		John Turner joins the company
1969	Bayford Glover formed	
1969	Thrust retail petrol brand launched	
1971		
1972		Fred Turner retires
1974		David and John Turner buy the company
1974		Shannon Houliston appointed general manager
1976	Whitfleet Ltd formed	
1977	Bayford (Developments) Ltd formed	
1979	Bayford Exploration formed	
1984	Bayford Exploration becomes Bayford Mining	
1984		Fred Turner dies
1984	Bayford invests in Fibresec	
1985	Group changes trading name to Bayford Energy	
1986	CEGB contract ends	
1986		Shannon Houliston leaves
1988		Jonathan Turner and Liz Slater join the company
1988	Bayford invests in PMD Technologies	
1988	Bowcliffe Hall becomes Bayford's headquarters	
1990	Cambria Fuels acquired	
1990	Bayford is partner in Hunslet Green regeneration scheme	
1991	Sale of Bayford Coal	
1991	Holderness Fuel Supplies acquired	
1992	Bayford sells stake in Fibresec	

Timeline

Date	Events	People
1993	Bayford becomes sole owner of Fleet Storage	
1993	Keighley Fuel Services acquired	
1993	First fuel card, Diesel Direct, launched	
1994	Bayford acquires 22 filling stations from Elf	
1995	Group changes trading name to Bayford Thrust	
1995	Bayford acquires Burmah Petroleum Fuels	
1996	The Gator is introduced	
1998	Thrust franchising scheme launched	
1999	Investors in People achieved	
1999		Jonathan Turner becomes commercial director and Liz Slater becomes sales director
2000	Bayford supplies leaded petrol to classic car enthusiasts	
2000	Bayford acquires Dominion Fuels from BP	
2000		Jonathan Turner becomes managing director
2001	Gulf brand licensed to Bayford and Gulf Lubricants and Gulf Retail formed	
2002	Save Group acquired by Jack Petchey and Jonathan Turner becomes joint managing director of Save Retail	
2003	Countrywide Fuel Cards launched	
2004		Jonathan Turner buys the company
2006	The Fuelcard Company UK plc launched	
2007		Jonathan Turner becomes chief executive and Liz Slater becomes managing director
2009	Bayford sells oil distribution businesses to DCC	
2011	The Right Fuelcard Company formed by Bayford and Rontec	
2013	Laudale Estate acquired by Jonathan Turner	
2015	Blackburn Wing completed	
2017	The Yorke Arms, Ramsgill, acquired by Jonathan Turner	
2018	Gulf Gas & Power plc set up in the UK and Gulf Gas & Power set up in the Netherlands	
2018		Lindsay Austin appointed managing director
2019	The Right Fuelcard Company sold to Edenred	
2019	Bayford begins investing in Fulcrum plc	
2020	Pandemic forces closure of Drivers' Club and the Yorke Arms	
2020	Bayford acquires E Gas & Electric	
2020	Bayford sets up Orange Disc Ltd	

Financial Statistics

Bayford & Co Ltd

YearEnding	Sales (£000s)	Net Profit/ Pre-Tax Profit (£000s)	Source
1945	72	2	Minute Book
1946	74	3	Minute Book
1947	69	3	Minute Book
1948	87	4	Minute Book
1949	94	1	Minute Book
1950	102	3	Minute Book
1951	121	4	Minute Book
1952	129	2	Minute Book
1953	135	3	Minute Book
1954	140	4	Minute Book
1980	35489	1383	John Turner
1981	40878	774	John Turner
1982	52310	1303	John Turner
1983	52990	1150	John Turner
1984	63685	1408	John Turner
1985	69751	1230	John Turner
1986	52507	487	John Turner
1987	37465	144	John Turner
1988	36804	-830	John Turner
1989	41089	216	John Turner
1990	46507	-449	John Turner
1991	50759	-218	John Turner
1992	45778	-159	John Turner
1993	55625	187	John Turner

Bayford & Co Ltd

YearEnding	Sales (£000s)	Net Profit/ Pre-Tax Profit (£000s)	Source
1994	70618	826	John Turner
1995	77349	48	John Turner
1996	113484	-958	John Turner
1997	110392	-250	John Turner
1998	109050	245	John Turner
1999	96950	293	John Turner
2000	108679	283	John Turner
2001	120061	211	John Turner
2002	161744	226	John Turner
2003	137323	482	Company Accounts
2004	191135	564	Company Accounts
2005	237355	1116	Company Accounts
2006	392135	2822	Company Accounts
2007	336132	936	Company Accounts
2008	452263	2084	Company Accounts
2009	411482	1384	Company Accounts
2010	141159	19566	Company Accounts
2011	1575	-295	Company Accounts
2012	2257	-93	Company Accounts
2013	1721	-64	Company Accounts
2014	2169	-241	Company Accounts
2015	121486	844	Company Accounts
2016	133740	2906	Company Accounts
2017	155698	865	Company Accounts
2018	17312	17511	Company Accounts
2019	3903	23521	Company Accounts

Note on Sources

The main sources for compiling the story of Bayford have been:

1   Minutes 1937–2008

2   Collected scrapbooks of press cuttings, 1950–

3   Miscellaneous press cuttings and articles

4   Miscellaneous company newsletters, 1980s–2000s

5   Interviews with Lindsay Austin, Ken Gardiner, Sally Genn, Tim Hall, David and Debbie Hobson, Mark Kilvington, Lorraine Lowe, Bob McNaughton, Julie O'Shaughnessy, Chris Ritchie, Tony Sharp, Liz Slater, James Spencer, Rob Staines, John Turner, Jonathan Turner and Karen Turner.

Index